The Liners

of

Liverpool

by

Derek M. Whale

Part II

X

Cover Design: ERIC R. MONKS

Acknowledgements

I thank all the copyright holders of photographs and illustrations in this book — especially the Liverpool Daily Post & Echo (whose pictures are acknowledged as D.P. & E.). And all those whom it has not been possible to trace, in particular, the cameramen of the last century, some of whose prints are now rare historic gems.

My thanks also to the following for their most helpful assistance:

Anchor Line (Mr. William Higgins); Bibby Line (Mr. Derek Bibby, M.C., Chairman); Booth Line and Lamport and Holt (Mr. Denis Ormesher); Canadian Pacific Public Relations Department (Miss Amanda Pollard and Mr. Peter Alhadeff); Mr. Craig Carter; Mr. John Crowley; Cunard Archives, University of Liverpool (Mr. Michael Cook and Miss Andrea Rudd); Furness Withy Group P.R. Department (Mr. Richard Alexander); Captain Harry M. Hignett; Merseyside Maritime Museum (Mr. Michael Stammers); Mr. Eric Munday; Ocean Transport and Trading (Miss Sally Furlong and Miss Jenny Lovatt); Pacific Steam Navigation Company (Mr. John Lingwood); Mr. Reginal Page — and my daughter, Helen Jane.

03602455

ddd

First published 1987 by Countyvise Limited, 1 & 3 Grove Road, Rock Ferry, Birkenhead, Wirral, Merseyside L42 3XS.

Copyright © Derek M. Whale, 1987.
Photoset and printed by Birkenhead Press Limited, 1 & 3 Grove Road, Rock Ferry, Birkenhead, Merseyside L42 3XS.

ISBN 0 907768 14 8

Contents

Foreword

by Michael Stammers
Assistant Director, Merseyside Maritime Museum

The great liners were so much part of the life of the port and the city of Liverpool that it is still hard to believe they have gone forever. Perhaps we almost took it for granted that there would always be a Cunarder or a Canadian Pacific ship tied up along the Landing Stage, busy with tugs, taxis and boat-trains.

Now, the whole scene has been transformed; the last liner sailed over a decade ago, the beloved Landing Stage has been sold for scrap and the famous Riverside Station, terminus of the boat-trains, stands derelict without its roof.

But though the last of the liners has gone, the people of Merseyside have not forgotten them. Indeed, many served aboard them and many more have watched their arrival and departure.

There are few Merseysiders without at least one relative, friend or ancestor who went to sea in the liners. So there are memories, many memories. Derek Whale has written not just a history of the ships but also recorded in print for future generations the stories, thoughts and feelings of the people who knew and sailed the liners.

It is as vital to preserve the oral history of our maritime heritage as it is to preserve the models, pictures, photographs and plans of the ships. I hope that Derek Whale will continue with more stories from the people of Merseyside's liner era.

Introduction

In Part One of The Liners of Liverpool, I presented a general background to the Merseyside Maritime scene from sail to steam.

This also included the once-great holders of the Blue Riband of the Atlantic — Mauretania the first and her ill-fated sister, Lusitania.

Parts Two and Three of the book contain individual stories of other famous Liverpool liners, which I have selected.

The stories of the ships are not in strict alphabetical chapter order. This is because, in some instances, a ship is given more than one name in her career. And, sometimes, I have mentioned more than one liner within a chapter.

Canadian Pacific's "White Empresses" have been given considerable space in this book, and a couple more will follow in Part Three. Because of the number of these, I have interspersed some with stories of ships from other lines.

However, all the ships' names appear alphabetically in the index for quick page reference.

Part III of The Liners of Liverpool will contain the following ships:—
Aba, Accra, Apapa, Aureol, Carinthia (Fairland/Fairsea), Caronia (Caribia), Delius, Derbyshire (II) and (IV), Devonshire, Empress of Ireland, Empress of Scotland (I) and (II), Hilary (III), Hildebrand (II) and (III), Hubert (III), Ivernia (Fraconia/Feodor Shalyapin), Lancastria, Mauretania (II), Newfoundland (I) and (II), Nova Scotia (I) and (II), Orduna, Reina del Mar, Reina del Pacifico, Saxonia (Carmania/Leonid Sobinov), Sylvania (Fairwind), Vandyck, Vestris, Voltaire.

Athenia and Letitia

One British ship had to suffer the horror of being the first to be sunk by enemy action in World War II and ensure its place in history. But which ship?

Certainly the master with the famous name, Captain James Cook, had no idea that the arrow of the wheel of fate had stopped and was pointing at his ship, the Athenia, as she embarked 1,417 passengers, including hundreds of Americans and Canadians, and crew, at Liverpool, bound for Canada, on September 2, 1939.

Like most of the big liners which crossed the North Atlantic regularly between the two world wars, Athenia and all who sailed in her had been blessed with peaceful passages since she was built at Fairfield's on the Clyde, for Anchor-Donaldson Line in 1923. A twin-screw liner of 13,465 tons, she made her maiden voyage from Glasgow to Quebec and Montreal on April 21 that year. Every month she would call at Liverpool and, for some time in 1923, she was the sole passenger liner on the Liverpool-Canada service, until Cunard's Carmania and Caronia joined in the following year.

The Cunarders reverted to the Liverpool-New York run in 1925, when Athenia was joined by her new running-mate, the Letitia. The sisters also made winter cruises in addition to their routine voyages to Halifax and St.John. They had replaced the steamers of the same names, which were lost in the Great War. Letitia I, which became a hospital ship, was wrecked near Halifax in August, 1917, and (shades of things to come), Athenia I was torpedoed by a U.boat in the same month. Anchor-Donaldson Line succumbed to the trade depression of the early 'Thirties', and when the company disbanded in 1935, Athenia and Letitia passed into the ownership of the Donaldson Atlantic Line.

As Athenia made her way to St.George's Channel and the open Atlantic that early September day, her passengers were apprehensive to say the least. With rumours of war so rife, there must have been a lot of praying for, or willing the lonely liner to a quick landfall, for the first ocean-bound convoy of the war was not formed until five days later, on September 7. Dull, unsettled weather with a south-easterly wind and occasional rain was the forecast. But for those like Captain Cook and his officers the gathering war clouds bore greater significance.

Next day, Sunday, September 3, 1939, war was declared. Athenia had but hours to live.

At about 7 o'clock that evening, the liner was 250 miles out into the Atlantic, north west of Ireland. Like his passengers, Captain Cook was having his dinner. It is doubtful whether he was enjoying it. More

Athenia. As the first British merchant ship to be sunk in the last world war, she made grim maritime history. (J.S. Clarkson)

than 1,500 souls and a huge and costly vessel in his charge and, as always, mountains of paperwork and a catalogue of decisions to make, was enough responsibility at the best of times. But now, this additional, unknown risk. . . . .

* * *

Hitler's submarines were at sea. Close to Athenia's course lurked U.30, in which podgy skipper Oberleutnant Fritz Lemp was stretching, having also just finished his dinner in his tiny wardroom.

"Surface ship sighted," he was told.

At 7.35 p.m., from a distance of 1,600 yards, Lemp ordered three torpedoes to be fired at the single-funnelled, blacked-out and unarmed ship, which he saw in his periscope. Struck deep abaft the port side of the engine-room by one of these, Athenia stopped, mortally wounded. There was no need for blackout now. Lights — those which could be switched on — lit up the target as if to proclaim her unarmed innocence.

She started to settle and list badly as hundreds of men, women and children crowded her bright decks. Attempts to lower the lifeboats proceeded at a feverish pace, although it took about an hour to evacuate the ship. Survivors said that the submarine surfaced and

Above: *The Letitia at anchor in the Mersey.*

Below: *Inward-bound from Montreal in August, 1935, the Letitia ran aground in thick fog near the entrance to Belfast Lough. Her passengers were taken off by tug and disembarked at Belfast.*

fired two shells at the liner as her crew helped passengers into the boats. One of the shells exploded on the middle deck.

The Norwegian tanker, Knute Nelson, nearest of the ships to hear Athenia's stuttering S.O.S., arrived at midnight, closely followed by the yacht, Southern Cross. The City of Flint also appeared and, by dawn, the three ships, aided by the British destroyers Fame, Electra and Escort, which joined in the rescue work, had collected more than 1,000 survivors from the sea.

But Lemp's torpedo had taken more than its toll of tonnage and among the 112 passengers and crew who died were 85 women and children. Some were killed in the first explosion and others perished in the sea. Ironically, some of Athenia's crew were survivors of World War One U.boat attacks.

There was a heavy swell that grim night, but the moon at least shone brightly. Lifeboats, burning flares, dotted the sea. Helping hands constantly reached out to the gasping, moaning figures in the water, but many sank before they would be dragged to safety. One woman, already sitting in a lifeboat, looking forlorn and dazed, suddenly leaped back into the sea, screaming "My baby . . . !" A lifeboat containing 52 women floated under the stern of the Knute Nelson, whose propeller tore the bottom out. A few were killed in this incident, but with the boat gone, only about another seven or eight eventually survived.

There was a marked contrast between the sinking of the Athenia and that of the sinking of the steamer Glitra, the first British merchant ship to be sunk in the Great War. Great Britain entered that war on August 4, 1914, but it was not until October 20 that Germany made this attack. And Glitra's crew at least were allowed to take to their boats, and only then was their steamer torpedoed and sunk. Initial chivalry died early in both wars and lies, the constant nourishment of propaganda, took its place.

According to a United Press report from London to America at this time, shortly before Athenia's survivors were landed at Greenock and Galway, Baron Ernst von Weizsaecker, Secretary of State of the German Foreign Office, assured Alexander C. Kirk, Chaire d'Affaires of the American Embassy, that the German Navy had no part in the disaster. The sweet smell of forthcoming congratulations for having carved himself a niche in navel history by sinking the first British ship in World War II, must have suddenly stunk under the nose of U.30's commander, when he saw that human freight scurrying about under the stricken liner's floodlights and had had time to absorb the frightfulness of what he had done.

If all is fair in love and war, then it is only fair to record that Oberleutnant Lemp was duly shocked and horrified by this action, which was not even admitted by Germany until after the war.

A brightly-lit Empire Brent (ex-Letitia), at Prince's Landing Stage, Liverpool, in 1946. D.P. & E.)

Letitia must have had her sister's share of luck, for she survived the war, serving as an armed cruiser and then as a transport. In 1944, she became a Canadian hospital ship, like her predecessor and, in 1946, she was purchased by the British Government for a troopship. Although her name was then changed to the unromantic Empire Brent, in 1952 she became the Captain Cook, an emigrant ship, and made her first chartered voyage in April, 1955.

The Captain Cook carried many thousands of emigrants in one-class passages from Britain to Australia and to New Zealand. She made her last trip in February, 1960, with servicemen from Singapore and Cyprus, having steamed 2½ million miles during her lifetime.

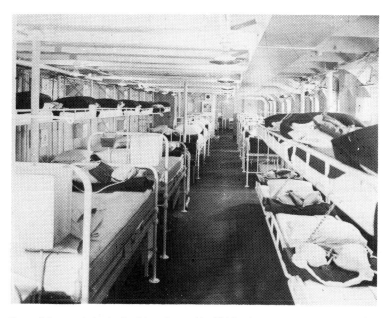

One of the wards in the Letitia, pictured in 1945, when returning war-wounded men to Canada. She was then described as the world's most modern floating hospital. (D.P. & E.)

Empress of Australia

Probably few of those who used to watch Canadian Pacific's three-funnelled Empress of Australia arriving and departing from Liverpool were aware that she was the ship which Kaiser Wilhelm II said, in World War One, that he intended to use as his personal yacht on a victory tour of the world.

... And that, on board this liner, he would accept the surrender of the British Fleet!

Still when the Great War was over, this fine vessel was surrendered to Britain at Hull by a German crew, and she spent all the rest of her life as a faithful servant of Britain, even up to some 11 years after the Kaiser's death, in June, 1941.

Launched by Vulkan, of Stettin, on December 20, 1913, as the luxury liner Tirpitz, she was intended for service with the Hamburg-Amerika Line. After some trooping for the British Government, she was bought from the Reparations Commission by Canadian Pacific on July 25, 1921. The company renamed the 21,833-ton liner Empress of China (III). But she never sailed under that name, which was changed to Empress of Australia (I) on June 2, 1922.

The loss of their big ships, as reparations to the Allies, was almost as bitter as losing the war to the Germans. Admiral von Tirpitz, after whom the Empress-to-be was named, angrily proclaimed in Berlin a month after the war:

·"German unity has been lost to the robbers who have only been lurking for an opportunity to filch Germany's flourishing prosperity away; who have robbed Germany of her old merchant fleet. . . ." Such are the fruits and frustrations of war.

During refitting, at Hamburg and Clydebank, her boilers were converted for oil-burning. Some of the crew instructions still remained printed in German!

She sailed on June 16, 1922, from the Clyde to Vancouver to begin her Pacific service between that port and Hong Kong, via Yokohama and Shanghai. At the time, she was the largest ship to pass through the Panama Canal. Of the shelter-deck type, she had a straight stem, eliptical stern, three funnels and two masts. She wrote a noble chapter of her history during this period, as a refuge ship at Yokohama when the Japanese earthquake started on September 1, 1923, and Tokyo was almost demolished.

Yokohama port was practically wiped out and more than 100,000 people perished. The land literally rippled in waves from 6ft. to 8ft. high. The port became an inferno and thousands of refugees streamed to the harbour, where even large vessels were being tossed

The Kaiser hoped to use the Tirpitz as his personal yacht. Instead, as the Empress of Australia (I), she carried British royalty! (Canadian Pacific)

around like corks. Small boats had to cross a sea of flaming oil in their rescue work. These included those from the Empress of Australia, which sent many of her crew ashore to render assistance and to return with victims. She became a hospital ship for the wounded and a sanctuary for the homeless.

The great seamanship of her master, Captain Samuel Robinson, at this nightmarish time, did not go unnoticed. He had guided the huge ship away from the demolished wharf and out of the flaming sea, even though the Empress's port propeller was out of action, fouled by a cable. Later, many deserving tributes were paid to him. He was also given the C.B.E. and awarded the Silver Medal of the Order of St.John of Jerusalem.

A New York banker's wife, one of the passengers on board at the time of the earthquake, wrote a graphic account of this action, including a tribute to Captain Robinson:

"He manoeuvred the ship most expertly, and, with all her handicap, managed to turn about and tack back and forth until she got out of the path of seething oil flames, which were threatening to destroy the boat and take with it the lives of all on board. There was no alternative except to take the risk of getting through the breakwater channel, which we finally did — another inexplicable miracle as the only part of the breakwater remaining intact were the entrance lights."

Likewise, Captain Robinson also paid tribute to the passengers who had remained so calm and who worked non-stop day and night attending to the injured. The passengers had a special bronze plaque made for the liner to commemorate the heroic actions of the Captain, his officers and crew.

In 1926/27, when the number of travellers between Britain and Canada started growing, Empress of Australia was re-engined and reconditioned at a cost of half a million pounds to make her into one of the most luxurious liners in the world.

The changed attitude of women going to sea in these days greatly influenced the architects and the designers in replanning her passenger accommodation. As someone said: "Instead of moping in deck-chairs for the greater part of the voyage, women afloat now want to be dancing or swimming, or otherwise energetically amusing themselves."

Canadian Pacific added the Empress to their Atlantic fleet and, she made her first voyage Southampton to Quebec on June 25, 1927. Among her passengers the following month were the Prince of Wales and the Prime Minister, Mr.Stanley Baldwin — two gentlemen who were not going to see eye-to-eye at the Abdication, a decade later. But on this occasion, with the Empress taking good care of them, they were on much more agreeable ground — on passage to Canada for the Diamond Jubilee of the Confederation.

With many world cruises behind her, twelve years later, on May 6, 1939, the Empress of Australia, carrying Edward's brother and successor, King George V1, and Queen Elizabeth, was described as "a floating palace". This, of course, referred to her Royal passengers but, in truth, her decor and furnishing would have graced a palace, anyway. Furniture from the Royal Yacht, Victoria and Albert, had been brought on board and placed in the royal apartments.

The liner's main lounge was decorated and designed Empire-style, with unobstructed floor space for dancing. The Louis X1V smoking-room had oak-pannelled walls, tapestries and leather-covered chairs and sofas. The drawing-room, after Louis XV1 period, was finished in white, with gold embellishments, and the main swimming-pool was designed like one from ancient Pompeii. Extending the full width of the ship, the dining-room was in French Regency style, fitted with small tables, with overall subdued lighting and individual table lamps.

Although a sailor himself, King George could not have been superstitious for, on Saturday, the 13th May, he sat in place No.13 at the liner's royal table for dinner!

Old sailors among the liner's crew, and other veterans, must have noted that the warship-escorted Empress on this almost prophetical voyage was fullfilling her curious historic mission with the King of

King George VI sat in seat no.13, on May 13, 1939, at this dining table, taken from the Royal Yacht, Victoria and Albert, and placed in the Empress of Australia for the royal visit to Canada.

Britain, in place of the Kaiser, using her as his personal yacht and accepting homage from abroad. The Empress also made mercantile history by flying the Royal Navy's White Ensign on this voyage.

Cruise ships, sailing as they often do in warm latitudes under starry skies and moonlit, smooth seas, tend to beckon Cupid and induce romance. But Empress of Australia must have set up something of a record during her 36,000-mile round-the-world cruise in 1928, when no fewer than 12 couples on board became engaged!

Like so many of the passenger liners which sailed through periods over five reigns, in the wake of Venus and of Mars, Empress of Australia was also a ship of love and war. She became a troopship in September 1939, and remained a transport vessel throughout the war and to the end of her days, long afterwards. Luckily, she sustained little more damage than being accidentally "holed" by the S.S.Ormonde at Oran.

In common with many of our famous ships during that war, she also had her turn of being "sunk" for enemy propaganda purposes. In January, 1941, the Germans claimed to have torpedoed, shelled and sunk her somewhere 200 miles off Dakar. This claim was later seen as having been a "Kite" flown to discover her true whereabouts

Spring, 1946, saw the Empress reconditioned, and she later continued as a transport with her troop decks reconverted to provide comfortable lounges for 700 officers and service families, and 1,000

Empress of Australia (I) battling through the rough North Atlantic in May, 1939. (Planet News)

other-ranks, making up her newly-allocated capacity. This compared with her often carrying 5,000 troops during the war and 3,000 on more recent voyages.

She added a little more to her history in March, 1948, by bringing home to Liverpool the last soldiers from India. But, in January, 1951, now aged 39, she was Britain's largest and oldest troopship.

Although a "grandmother" in terms of ships' lives, Empress of Australia was still given a year's reprieve from the breakers because of the disturbed international situation and the "Cold War". Already up for sale, she made her 70th and final voyage as a troopship on February 17, 1952, when she sailed from Liverpool with serviceman and their families to the Far East, to the strains of "Auld Lang Syne", played by a military band. She might have survived for a few more years had any of the attractive offers made by foreign buyers been snapped up, but, because of the acute steel shortage in the country, Canadian Pacific decided to sell her to the British Iron and Steel Corporation.

Returning home to Liverpool, the old girl kicked out in a truly memorable last fling, breaking all her speed records, on the last leg of her passage up the Irish Sea by averaging 17½ knots. She arrived at Liverpool on April 30.

Do ships' officers and men really feel sad when a vessel, which generally has served them well, comes home to die? The answer, of course, is a definite Yes. Off Point Lynas, the outward-bound

16

Empress of Canada passed the Australia, now close to home with her last passengers — 2,700 servicemen and families. The Canada's master signalled: "My ship's company join me in saluting you all on the final voyage of a very gallant and famous ship." Captain L.C. de Hauteville Bell, master of the Empress of Australia, replied: "The day has come at last."

The people of a great port like Liverpool, who followed the careers of these famous ships with genuine interest, also shared their passing with as much tenderness as those directly concerned with them. And there were many sad faces on Merseyside on May 8, 1952, as Empress of Australia sailed from the Mersey for the breaker's yard at Inverkeithing.

Poignant was the little message flashed to her from an inward-bound Norwegian freighter, reading: "Farewell, good ship." Captain de Hauteville Bell, still in command on this last voyage, replied simply: "Thank you."

Seldom is a ship demolished without souvenirs being taken, but pride of place among those removed from the Empress of Australia must go to the plaque commemorating the liner's merciful assistance at Yokohama - and, of course, her bell. These were presented to her retired former master, Captain Robinson, then living in Vancouver.

Berengaria

Hitler, it is said, used to bite carpets in some of his rages.

Kaiser Wilhelm 11 may not have resorted to such alarming displays, but when the Allies put him on the carpet at the end of the Great War and made Germany forefeit its ships over 1,600 tons to compensate for the allied tonnage it had sunk, his anger knew no bounds. The loss of Germany's big ships was one thing, the Kaiser's loss of face another. Among the tonnage was the huge liner which he personally had launched — the 52,226-ton Imperator.

She had two suites, known. as the Imperial suites, the most luxurious apartments to be found in any vessel afloat at that time. It is doubtful if the Kaiser or the Kaizerin ever used these, but his pride must have been sorely hurt when, later, they were used by British Royalty.

The Imperator sailed on her maiden voyage from Hamburg to New York on June 18, 1913, and in its July, 1913, issue, the magazine "Engineering", describing the new liner, told of "safety precautions

Berengaria . . . built as Germany's Imperator, she was the Kaiser's pride and joy. (Central News)

gone mad". "In addition to the commodore," it stated, "the ship carries four captains, who have commanded large steamers successfully, and one of these will always be on watch while the fourth takes general control of the crew. There are, in addition, seven officers, each of whom carries a captain's ticket, so that, as far as vigilance and skill can guarantee immunity from accident, there should be nothing to fear . . . . There is also a 30,000 candle-power searchlight on the foremast . . . ."

Imperator, renamed Berengaria, built her great reputation as a passenger liner by courtesy of Cunard and not the Kaiser. For it was to Cunard and the White Star Line that she and the Bismarck (which became the Majestic) were purchased, respectively, as suitable reparations for the losses of the Lusitania and the four-funnelled Britannic. Ironically, the liner, built at Hamburg in 1913 for the Hamburg-Amerika Line, with the Vaterland (which became America's Leviathan) and the Bismarck, had been planned as Germany's reply to Cunard and White Star in the lucrative and expanding North Atlantic passenger trade.

In Germany, in 1913, it was reported that to moor the Imperator, a special buoy, weighing 20 tons and with a circumference of 75 feet, had been made. This was the largest buoy in the world at the time.

Imperator, herself, carrying 3,000 passengers and a crew of 1,000, for a short time qualified as the largest liner in the world, although Bismarck was to hold this record for 19 years. At 900 feet, Imperator was also the longest ship.

So keen was the prestige among the competing shipping companies that when Cunard announced that, on completion, its new liner, Aquitania, would be 901 feet long, Germany hurriedly masted a huge bronze eagle figurehead on to Imperator's bow to add 17 extra feet to her length! Clutched in the eagle's talons was a globe carrying the company's motto, "Mein Feld is die Welt". A gale clipped off the eagle's wings and the liner soon came home to sit out the war. Imperator was also top heavy and, to prevent her listing, nine feet was lopped off each of her three funnels. The Germans also poured concrete into her, to which Cunard later added even more ballast of pig-iron.

Cunard made no major alterations to this lovely liner. It did, however, remove all numbers 13 from cabin doors (passengers can be just as superstitious as sailors) and replaced all the marble baths in her first-class cabins with metal ones to improve her stability.

Her internal decor was rich and beautiful, with elegancy given rein even to the extent of a Pompeiian swimming pool, with underwater lighting, marble seats and fountains. The smoke-room was a replica of an old English inn, with timbered ceiling and stag horns over a large, open fireplace. The main lounge, with a mainly-glass roof, extended almost the full width of the ship.

Berengaria at sea. With the Mauretania and the Aquitania, she helped to provide "the fastest ocean service in the world".
(Liverpool University Archives)

A delightful night study of Berengaria at Southampton, in March, 1930.
(Fox Photos)

"It was hard to believe you were at sea when you entered this lovely lounge, " said Mr. Reginald Page, of Wallasey, Merseyside, who spent six years as an engineer officer in the Berengaria, and to whom I am indebted for a considerable amount of first-hand information about this historical ship.

Reg, born on December 12, 1899, lost his only brother, James, in the Thetis submarine tragedy, when she sank when on trials in Liverpool Bay, in June, 1939. This was sheer fate. James, a fitter with Cammell Laird's, Birkenhead, who built Thetis, took the place of a colleague who had been taken ill.

Tropical plants, growing in brass-bound tubs, flourished in the warm atmosphere of the Berengaria's Palm Court and ballroom, which shared the same deck, and made a grand setting for the richly-gowned lady passengers. The dining-room, with gallery, could accommodate most of the first-class passengers at one sitting. And, of course, the fabulous dinners were always accompanied by the ship's orchestra.

When converted to oil, Berengaria had 48 boilers and her engine-room was attended by 14 engineers on each four-hour watch. With the two chief engineers, there were some 44 personnel.

Describing the liner's first voyage across the Atlantic from Southampton to New York after her conversion, Mr. Page recalled the operation of the large brass wheels, which controlled the speed and direction of the turbine-driven propellers from the "starting platform" as this was known. Two engineers manipulated each of these wheels and the officers used to observe a picture-plan of the turbines, steam-pipes, and so on, in which the turbines would be illuminated as the relevant valves were opened. "It was quite a sight to see twelve engineers controlling the steam to the turbines, which developed 70,000 horse-power," he said.

"Although the heat was intense, etiquette demanded that semi-full dress uniform be worn. The chief engineer, who was always present on these occasions, wore full-dress uniform.

"As we passed down the River Solent at slow speed, the ship made an impressive sight and, on rounding the Calshot Spit, we passed between Southsea and the Isle of Wight. Here, we increased speed, but with caution, as on one occasion our bow-wave struck Southsea beach and washed holidaymakers from their deck-chairs!"

Admiring New York on that first memorable voyage, Reg told how he visited the Capital Picture House, at that time the largest and finest in the world. "In between the showing of films, the stage would rise from below with an orchestra of over 100 musicians in place and ready to play." This was at the time of the Prohibition and, said Reg, ships' officers were allowed to purchase three bottles of whisky during each voyage and some of them sold these to Press photographers who came on board at quarantine. Those who did made sufficient cash to cover their expenses during the ship's stay in New York.

"I had a chemist friend, who owned a drug store in Harlem, and whenever my shipmates and I visited him he would produce a large bottle of rye whisky and tell us to help ourselves. On one of these occasions, we were joined by the local traffic cop and his sergeant. Seeing this, it would not have surprised us if the chief of police had also turned up for the party!

"Once, during our stay in New York, we had a visitor who claimed to be the mayor of a small mining town. After he had consumed several tots of Scotch, he emptied his pockets of small change and threw this into a waste-paper basket. When he had sobered up a bit, we took him over the ship's staterooms and, on seeing the old English smoke-room, he was so impressed that he cried. He said that it reminded him of his poor old mother. Later, he told us that he had his own still for making whisky at the bottom of his garden, and that when the cask was full, the cops came to his house and carried this into his cellar."

Visiting a New York "speak-easy", via a tortuous route of passages and doors, Reg said that he found himself in a room like a pub, with fully-fitted bar, tables and waiter-service. "My American friend pointed out to me several men there whom he knew held high offices in the city," he said . . . . so much for the drinking ban!

* * *

Some weeks after the Imperator came to Liverpool, after being handed over to Cunard by the Ministry of Shipping, she made her first voyage from the port to New York. That was on February 21, 1920. She originally had four classes of passenger accommodation but Cunard reduced this to three.

Cunard renamed Imperator as Berengaria after Richard Coeur de Lion's queen. She made her first voyage under that name on April 16, 1921, on the Southampton-New York run and proudly remained as the company's flagship until the legendary Queen Mary arrived to replace her.

The following year, Cunard was declaring that Berengaria, Aquitania and Mauretania were providing "the fastest ocean service in the world". At high cost, though, for Berengaria, at that time, was consuming 750 tons of fuel a day — twice that of the larger Queen Mary, which took her place. But her voracious capacity for coal was not fully met, according to one of her former stokers, Mr. John

Storey, of Liverpool, who was among the crew which sailed to New York in the Carmania to bring Imperator to England for the first time.

John and his colleagues found that they had to live in hostels and wait three months before the liner was released. They were given three dollars a day and some of them took on extra jobs, like trucking fruit. "We sailed home in the Imperator in December, 1918, and it took us 11½ days to reach Southampton," said John. "Whatever the Germans did to her while she was interned in New York, I doubt if anybody will ever know, but her German captain said that if she had Liverpool firemen in her, then nothing on the water would ever catch her!"

The wealth of many of the first-class passengers in these luxury liners must have made most of their crews feel as poor as church mice, because sailors' pay in those days, and for many years to come, was very low. One can imagine, therefore, the delight of John Storey, when he touched lucky one day in 1912, when working as a 14-years-old galley boy on the White Star tender, Magnetic, ferrying passengers to and from the company's liners anchored in the Mersey at Liverpool. An American, his wife and son, being transported to the landing stage from the huge Olympic, asked John for drinks of water. John brought these, ice-cold, and repeated the order on request. Handing back the glasses, the grateful American pressed two gold sovereigns into John's hand. "Get some sweets for yourself," said the man. John's eyes popped. "I'd never seen that much money, to call my own, in all my life," he said. And as for buying himself sweets with this sum, he could have bought 960 half-penny lollipops!

For scores of thousands of regular North Atlantic travellers, Berengaria was their favourite liner. She sailed at a time when movie-making was a fast-growing, giant industry, and there were so many American film-stars on board her for one trip that she was dubbed "Hollywood afloat". Passenger-travel by air was still in its infancy in the 'Twenties and 'Thirties, and the North Atlantic liners carried practically all of the famous personalities, from all walks of life, including royalty, who commuted between Britain and the U.S. and Canada. It was Berengaria which carried the body of the world-renowned crime-fiction author, Edgar Wallace, home from Hollywood, where he had been writing the script for one of the biggest box-office draws of the 'Thirties — "King Kong". The liner arrived at Southampton with her ensign at half-mast.

Another character who (up to the time of writing) had kept the world agog for half a century with her persistent claim to be the long-lost Grand Duchess Anastasia, youngest and only surviving daughter of Czar Nicholas II of Russia, Anna Anderson was smuggled into America in the Berengaria in 1928. She went there as a

23

guest of a Mrs. Leeds, but she returned to Berlin some years later to lay claim to the Czar's fortune which, it is said, is in the custody of the Bank of England.

Reg Page remembers many personalities who travelled in the Berengaria. Folk like America's Gertrude Ederle, the first woman to swim the English Channel, who received a great welcome on her arrival in New York. "A tug came out to meet us with a crowd of straw-hatted men on board, who shouted and cheered us all the way up the Hudson River," he said.

And Helen Wills, the tennis player, dubbed "Miss Poker Face," on her way home after winning the Women's Tennis Championship at Wimbledon . . . .

"I remember how, on arriving at quarantine, the Press photographers persuaded Helen to go on to the boat-deck for a picture," says Reg. "She sat on a ventilator and one hard-boiled cameraman lifted up her dress to display more than a little leg; but Helen pulled her dress down again. Undaunted, the photographer again lifted her dress, but Helen pulled it down. And so, the picture of little 'Poker Face' was taken."

A ship which might appear to be faultless to its passengers is not necessarily so regarded by its crew. Mr. Kenneth Longbottom, of Hooton, Cheshire, told me that the Berengaria was loathed by her engine-room staff because one of her turbine castings was apt to leak steam and created Turkish-bath conditions. Men often went sick with the complaint dubbed "Berengaria Back," he said. Also, she was known as a "workhouse", and sometimes complainants in the fleet were awarded a stint in the Berengaria!

"When the Majestic, the former Bismarck and eight years younger than the Berengaria, was sold out of service, this left Berengaria to consort the Queen Mary until the Queen Elizabeth arrived," said Mr. Longbottom. "The excuse was that the Majestic's split uptakes, allowing for more spacious public rooms, caused a structural weakness. Yet the Majestic, capable of 26 knots, weathered many terrible Atlantic storms. Berengaria later was banned from New York as a fire hazard and this saved the gallant Aquitania from the scrapyard."

Some of the best anecdotes concerning the great personalities carried by Berengaria are told of the former Prince of Wales, the late Duke of Windsor. In his book, "The Liners", Terry Coleman tells how, one midnight in the early 1930's, the Prince crept on board Berengaria when she was tied up at Southampton. With him was a ragtime band, called the "Blackbirds", which he personally conducted in the liner's great ballroom.

An astounded officer of the watch walked into the ballroom in time to hear the Prince conduct the last tune. He then asked the Prince why he had chosen the liner for this event. Said the Prince: "It was very convenient, of course, and — well, I thought we shouldn't be disturbed. Sometimes, you know, it's very hard to find a place where you can be alone."

After the Prince met Wallis Simpson, privacy for him must have been harder than ever to acquire. But one does wonder how protocol, security and discipline were exercised on the liner that night!

It was the Prince of Wales who produced the highlight of Reg's career with Berengaria. This was on a voyage to New York, and the Prince was occupying the Kaiser Suite — specially refurnished at Southampton. "I missed seeing the Prince come on board, but later in the day I donned my uniform and made my way up to the promenade deck," said Reg. "I saw the Prince as he walked quickly, cap in hand, around the deck. With him was Colonel Trotter, his constant companion during the voyage.

"The Prince wore a check-patterned suit and suede shoes. He was full of energy and kept up a steady pace. It was five times around the deck to the mile and the Prince certainly put in some mileage as one

Tugs aid the popular liner, once dubbed "Hollywood Afloat".

(Associated Press)

25

companion after another joined him and fell out, apparently exhausted. His companions included Lord Mountbatten and Duff Cooper, who became the War Minister, and the Prince kept going until the bugler sounded 'The Roast Beef of Old England', when it was time to dress for dinner.

"The next day, I strolled on to the boat-deck and found the royal party about to have a game of tug-of-war. I stood near a lifeboat as the Prince took off his coat and placed it on the canvas covering. He stood in his shirtsleeves and then took his place at the rope. As the teams took the strain, he was laughing at Duff Cooper's wife, who was patting her husband's posterior, telling him to 'keep it in'. I do not remember which side won, but the Prince dropped the rope and was convulsed with laughter. He walked over to where I stood and after putting on his jacket, he took out his cigarette case, offered me one and said: 'I couldn't pull for laughing'. He was a great sport.

"For this particular voyage we had more than the usual number of American heiresses, most of them looking forward to the night of the fancy-dress ball and hoping to dance with the Prince. On the night of the dance, the Prince had as his partner a lady of the royal party, and they joined in the dancing without fancy dress. But during the evening, I saw them leave the floor through a small door at the rear of the ballroom and shortly afterwards they both reappeared, dressed up as Apaches. They danced again together, and during the final parade, in front of the judges, they were awarded a prize amid great applause. The following dance was a Paul Jones, and all the American heiresses lined up expectantly, hoping to be favoured by partnering the Prince. The Prince, however, did not oblige, much to their disappointment, and he left the floor with his lady friend.

"When the ship's concert was held the next night, the Prince sat at a table with friends, including Lord and Lady Mountbatten. There were several turns, including the chief steward, a Welshman, who had a good tenor voice. The ship's company knew that he needed little encouragement to keep singing on the stage, and I think that the Prince had been told this beforehand and that he decided in advance the action which he took. When the chief steward appeared, the Prince gave him an over-enthusiastic welcome — or so I thought. At the end of the first song, the Prince applauded vigorously and the audience joined in. I noticed that the Prince bent his head to look at the programme and that he also had a grin on his face.

"This excessive applause was repeated after the chef had given his encore, and again after his third song. He finished by singing the Stoker's Song — 'Take your hats off, take your boots off, to the dirty old grimy stoker'. I think that someone then intervened. Although the Prince applauded enthusiastically, the singer did not reappear. The Prince had had his little joke and was thoroughly enjoying himself!"

In January, 1932, an uncle on the Berengaria must have had quite a surprise when the chief technical operator of the liner Olympic telephoned Berengaria with a message of love for him from his small nephew, Judah Nacovitch, of Whitechapel, London. This came about during the Telephone Exhibition at the Imperial Institute, when Judah was one of 18 children selected to hold telephone conversations with the Olympic, on passage to New York.

Two years earlier, on February 4, 1930, the Olympic — giant sister of the Titanic — made history when a 10-minute wireless-telephone conversation took place between the liner and White Star Line's head office in London, 1,500 miles away. This, it was claimed, was the first time such a conversation had been held between a shore office and a vessel at sea. It is doubtful, however, if the liner's operator ever before or after dealt with such a spate of messages and requests as he was subjected to by the exhibition kids in 1932. Questions ranged from What is the name of the Captain? and How long is the boat? to Have you had your tea? and Have you been sea-sick? . . . .

There are folk around today (in the mid 1980's), still cruising and commuting on ocean liners, who still remember similar voyages in the old Berengaria. People like retired builder Mr. George M. Cross, of New York, whom I met on board the fabulous QE 2 on a cruise to the Atlantic Islands, who made his first transatlantic crossing in Berengaria in 1922, followed by trips and world cruises in dozens of other famous long-gone British liners.

And Miss Helen Brownlee, also of New York, who made her first voyage in Berengaria in the early 'Thirties. A Cunard enthusiast of the first degree, she had made 67 voyages, including world cruises, when I spoke with her in 1977. Her father, the late William B. Brownlee, was in charge of gold shipments, and he and his family lived in the Cunard building on Broadway for 25 years. "Dad used to say that there'll always be an England and there will always be Cunard," said Helen.

* * *

In 1938, Berengaria was partly dismantled at Jarrow, and during the last war she served as an accommodation ship for seamen. She was finally scrapped on the Firth of Forth in 1946.

Let Mr. Page give her his own epitaph . . . . "Other great ships have been built since the Berengaria, but few have excelled her in refinements and seaworthiness. She truly was a Queen Of The Sea."

Empress of Britain (II)

When the 42,500-ton Empress of Britain was launched at John Brown's yard, Clydebank, on June 11, 1930, she was the largest vessel of Canadian Pacific's fleet of 78, and the biggest ship to ply between any two ports of the British Empire. At the time, she was the last word in luxury among the first-class transatlantic passenger liners and, befittingly, she was named and launched by the Prince of Wales, then Master of the Merchant Navy. The Prince also saw her depart on her maiden voyage from Southampton to Quebec on May 27, the following year.

Although he may not have realised it, the Prince of Wales that day demonstrated the speed superiority of aircraft over ships, which eventually led to the demise of our great passenger liners. In the first place, he had flown from Hendon to Hamble in his own Puss Moth bi-plane, so that he could inspect the ship before she sailed. On leaving the liner, obviously very impressed, and having told the Captain as he left the gangway: "My only regret is that I am not sailing, too!" he took a powerful speed-boat to Hythe. There, he boarded Imperial Airways' 15-ton, four-engined flying-boat, Satyrus, and handling the controls himself, piloted her out over the sea.

As the Empress moved into the Solent, the flying-boat roared overhead at 100 m.p.h. and dipped her wings in salute at almost masthead height. Among the hundreds of waving passengers were Hollywood's famous screen sweethearts, "Mary and Doug" — Mary Pickford and Douglas Fairbanks. "Business reasons" had ended their British holiday. The aircraft made another flypast, saluted and returned to base.

The Prince loved speed. On landing, he sped off in a motor launch to Hamble's R.A.F. training school, left in his own plane for Walton Heath, played in the White Club Golf Competition, and then raced off to London in a fast car. . . .

Empress of Britain the second was the third Atlantic giant to be built by Brown's. The first was the 32,000-ton Lusitania, launched in 1907, and then fastest ship in the Atlantic service, and the second, Aquitania (46,000 tons), the largest in this service.

In the launching speech, broadcast to the nation and to Canada, the Prince of Wales called the event important in the history of British shipbuilding and Empire shipping. The tonnage built by Canadian Pacific during the last three years constituted a record unparalleled in the history of the mercantile marine. There was romance in the story of the Canadian Pacific Railway, he said, and the listeners should give a thought to those early Empire builders, spanning an overwhelming continent with a line of steel, and driving their way relentlessly through from ocean to ocean.

The Prince of Wales (later the uncrowned King Edward VIII) pictured at John Brown's Shipyard, Clydebank, on June 11, 1930, on the occasion of his launching Empress of Britain II. (Canadian Pacific)

It was a memorable day. The Prince even managed to fit in a round of golf at East Renfrewshire Golf Club. Only one incident marred the occasion — a local boy, anxious to get a good view of the launch, climbed on to the roof of a building overlooking the yard, fell through a skylight and was killed.

Costing £3 million — a fortune then — Empress of Britain could carry 1,195 passengers and a crew of 713. Her four propellers were the biggest in the world; the two inner ones with a diameter of 19ft. 3ins., each weighed $25\frac{1}{2}$ tons. The outer props were detachable so that the liner could sail as a twin-screw ship when cruising — at an ample 18 knots.

The interior of the new ship was as magnificent as her outward lines. Small wonder that she was called "Mayfair afloat". Her ballroom had a dome studded with illuminated stars and planets, showing their positions in the sky as on the day she was launched. Heath Robinson, a brilliant and whimsical artist of the 'Twenties and 'Thirties, whose humerous sketches of bizarre, mechanical contraptions (which, I am told, could really work, and which were even printed on toilet-rolls to amuse captive readers!), designed the liner's cocktail-bar. Here, Robinson had depicted the evolution of the cocktail, as he imagined it, and where, we are informed, "frequenters could let their imaginations run riot in a rosy haze amid the fantastic humour of that artist". Her Olympian swimming-pool was the largest in any liner.

As Douglas Fairbanks said to the Press on the Empress's arrival in Canada, he found two "faults": "The voyage was too short because of the many attractions the ship offered, and the second was that those same attractions robbed one of the sense of being on an ocean voyage!"

The Empress came to Liverpool before her maiden voyage, arriving in the Mersey early on April 8, 1931, looking a picture with her white hull and three large buff funnels, the aftermost a dummy (in the top of which the ship's orchestra would practise!).

Liverpool, in fact, was harbouring another fine new liner at this time in Pacific Steam Navigation Company's Reina del Pacifico, which sailed on her maiden voyage a day later.

Pilot J.M. Berry skilfully eased the Empress into the dock, where she had come for hull scraping and painting prior to returning to Scotland for officially handing over to CPR. Her master was Captain R.G. Latta, of Heswall, who had formerly commanded the Empress of Australia. Captain Latta was made Commodore of the C.P. fleet at a special V.I.P. maiden-voyage dinner in Quebec on June 2.

Empress of Britain constantly broke her own records and, in August, 1933, she set up a new record for the Canadian service by

"Superstars" of the 'Twenties and early 'Thirties, Douglas Fairbanks, senior, and his wife, Mary Pickford, pictured on their arrival at Southampton in April, 1924, during their world tour. In films, swashbuckling Fairbanks generally sported a moustache. The couple, in public, used to draw bigger crowds than the President of the United States! (Central News)

steaming from Father Point to Cherbourg breakwater in 4 days 7 hours 32 minutes at an average speed of 24.93 knots.

This Empress was a great favourite of Edward, Prince of Wales, but his brother, who took over the Throne on Edward's abdication, and Edward's royal sister-in-law (they became King George VI and Queen Elizabeth), will always be associated with this liner, too. Shortly before the last war, in the early summer of 1939, the King and Queen sailed to Canada in the Empress of Australia for their tour of that country and also part of the United States. Homeward-bound in mid-June, they travelled in the specially-converted Empress of Britain from Newfoundland, Britain's oldest colony.

On leaving the tiny fishing village of Portugal Cove to make courtesy calls on their three escorting cruisers, HMS Berwick, HMS Glasgow and HMS Southampton, they boarded a ferry-boat, intending to sail part of the way out to HMS Glasgow, first on the list. Because of a strong wind, this warship had been ordered to leave the other cruisers and the Empress of Britain, and meet the ferry some five miles across the bay. As the Glasgow neared, the King and Queen and their party were transferred to a small naval launch to go alongside the cruiser. The sea was rough and suddenly the launch's engines stopped. Its propellers had become entangled in a fishing net.

The small boat and its ultra-VIP passengers simply drifted helplessly for some time until another naval boat dashed up to help. King George jumped on board this boat and took the Queen's hand to help her across. When alongside the Glasgow, they climbed up the companionway to the deck.

If those present thought that one episode where Royal persons were at risk was enough, then they underestimated the Sailor King (and his equally courageous Queen), for the couple re-embarked in a swell-tossed launch again and headed for the cruiser Southampton. The sea crashed over the small boat and soaked all on board. And there simply wasn't enough room for everybody to jam into the little cabin.

Smiling and cheerful, the royal pair visited HMS Southampton and then continued to fulfil their promise by visiting the Berwick. They were still wet when they returned to the Empress of Britain, which must have seemed like a palace after their ordeal.

It was bad weather such as they had experienced (Captain C.S. Sapsworth cut the liner's speed from 24 to 20 knots to make life more comfortable), that prompted the King to cancel the Home Fleet's planned "welcome home" for them.

As if to cap the distressing day in which they had put on their brave faces, the King and Queen arrived on board the liner to learn that an able seaman, named Batt, had fallen overboard and drowned. They requested that the usual shipboard evening's filmshow be cancelled

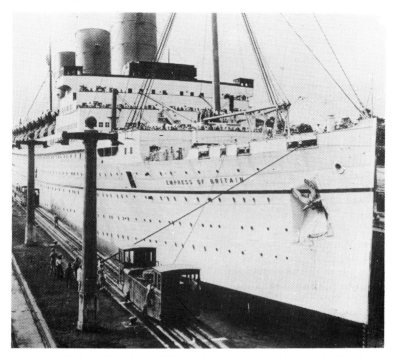

Empress of Britain II – dubbed "Mayfair afloat" and a great favourite among her passengers who included Royalty.

and that no music be played. And they sent a personal message of sympathy to the unfortunate seaman's mother. As the liner sailed out of the iceberg zone, the King and Queen attended divine service, conducted by Staff Captain Grant. With the war clouds then gathering, they also prayed for peace. And they said a special prayer for A/B Batt.

This was a momentous voyage for the Empress of Britain. Outward-bound from Liverpool for New York at this time was Cunard's new Mauretania II on her maiden voyage. Messages of goodwill were exchanged between the King and Queen and the new liner.

Like any good parents, the King and Queen were looking forward to being greeted at Southampton by their daughters, Princess Elizabeth and Princess Margaret Rose, and the Queen spent ten minutes chatting to them by wireless/telephone, linking her cabin with London. Empress of Britain was the first vessel in which an international telephone service was available from passengers' rooms.

There was nothing to distinguish commoner from royalty when, at Southampton, accompanied by their grandmother, Queen Mary, the little Princesses dashed up the gangway to hug their parents, with cries of "Hello, Mummy", and "Hello, Daddy". Dad got three kisses!

Two of the liner's smallest pages, Douglas Mackay, of Liverpool, and Robert Clint, of Southampton, both aged 15, presented two huge toy pandas to the Princesses. Every man-Jack of the liner's crew had contributed towards these.

Mr. John (Jack) Shaw, brother of the late author, Frank Shaw, Liverpool's most famous writer of "Scouse" stories, sailed in a number of the renowned pre-war liners, with long service in the Empress of Britain. A ship's butcher, Jack was known as "the birdman" of Canadian Pacific, for whenever a migratory bird, or racing pigeon, fell exhausted to the deck of the liner, it was always Jack who cared for it.

"Racing pigeons, of course, could be easily identified by the rings they wore," said Jack. "I would release these when we reached home. As butcher, I had charge of all animals and birds, be these the property of passengers or merely birds in distress. It was always 'take them to Jack Shaw'. Jeannette MacDonald, the lovely red-haired film star singer, left her collie with me on one voyage. I used to talk to her each day when I exercised the dog."

Jack remembers meeting many famous passengers on the Empress of Britain, one of whom was Jim Mollison, the crack flier and husband of the equally-famous ace pilot, Amy Johnson. "Jim visited my shop on board and a young assistant asked him for his autograph," Jack told me. "He had just obliged, when the lad asked Jim if he could also let him have his wife's autograph. . . . 'Yes, if you want me to commit bloody forgery', smiled Jim, who promptly wrote down Amy's name, which was eagerly received by the collector!"

Jack met the illustrious playwright, George Bernard Shaw, on the liner's world cruise in 1932. Shaw had constantly refused to be photographed with passengers but finally consented to having his picture taken with some of the crew when asked by pressmen at Shanghai. He hand-picked the men, a well-assorted bunch, many from Merseyside and smaller than himself, so that only the chef's tall hat competed with the famous Shavian head!

Jack recalls this picture, in which he also should have appeared. "I had the feeling that Shaw did not like the butchery trade, but he was very pleasant to me," said Jack. "Unfortunately, I was below when this historic picture was taken. But GBS did sign one of the prints: 'To one Shaw from the Other'."

"Shaw was a great guy, who had been an amateur boxer in his youth and was well known in London's amateur clubs," said Jack,

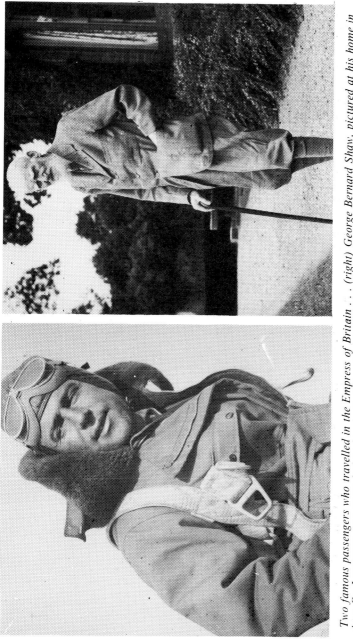

Two famous passengers who travelled in the Empress of Britain ... (right) George Bernard Shaw, pictured at his home in Ayot St. Lawrence, two years before his death. (Graphic Photo Union). (left) Jim Mollison, arriving at Croydon Airport in 1936, in his plane, "Miss Dorothy", after a record Atlantic crossing. ("Topical" Press Agency).

once a dedicated amateur boxer himself. "He would have continued with this sport, but was too tall and not heavy enough.". On board, he refused to 'dress for dinner', and would sit in the dining-room in sloppy clothes, reading a book propped up on the table. Mrs.Shaw was a very quiet lady.

"We had the British Olympic team on board, going to Los Angeles, and walking champion, Tommy Green, used to train by walking quickly round and round the deck early every morning. As a keep-fit fanatic himself, GBS was in the habit of trotting around the deck at the same time. I used to think it very funny to watch GBS, with his long legs, passing Tommy, with the greeting: 'Morning, Green', and Tommy's reply: 'Morning, sir' — and that would be all they had to say!"

Shaw was treated like royalty wherever he went and he received a great welcome in the States. This famous man died in November, 1950 — at the venerable age of 94.

CPR's crack flagship's voyages were numbered after she left Britain for Canada the day before the declaration of war. On arrival at Quebec she exchanged her lovely white dress for drab war-grey. She was part of the first convoy to carry Canadian troops to Britain. Other great liners in this convoy included the Empress of Canada, the Aquitania, Andes, Empress of Japan, Mauretania — and the giant Queen Mary. These seven luxury liners added up to an unequalled wartime convoy record of 276,918 tons — officially listed as US 3, but dubbed "The Multi Million Dollar" convoy.

Unlike her predecessor, the 1906-built Empress of Britain (renamed Montroyal in 1923), which survived the Great War through which she carried troops to all parts of the world and was attacked at least a dozen times, Empress of Britain (II) had a short war record. Although she spent a good deal of her time operating out of Southampton, it was from Liverpool that she began her final voyage. That was on August 6, 1940, when she was scheduled to make a round trip to Suez via Capetown.

Homeward-bound, clear of the Azores and some 70 miles from Ireland in the north-west approaches to Liverpool, she was bombed on the morning of October 26 by a four-engined German aircraft. There were some direct hits. One bomb cut right through her top deck, penetrating and setting fire to her lovely Mayfair Lounge and causing destruction on the lower decks. Then another high-explosive bomb hit her, together with a shower of incendiaries.

The only man on board with a real bird's-eye view of this holocaust was Able Seaman Jim Carroll, of Liverpool, who was in the crow's-nest when the aircraft swooped to almost mast-height to bomb the ship. Jim actually saw a bomb leave the plane and strike the Empress.

But what sort of defence could the Empress put up with one 3-inch gun and four Lewis guns, firing "rifle" ammunition? Abandoned and burning, she was later taken in tow in the hope that she could reach land. Two destroyers stood by as escorts. She was just a sitting duck for U.boats. And, sure enough, in the darkness of the early hours of October 28, Leutenant Commander Jenisch sank her with two torpedoes from U.32.

She was the largest merchant ship to be sunk during the war and 49 of her complement died. Of a total of 643 passengers — militia and their families — and crew on board, 598 were rescued. Her master, Captain Charles Howard Sapsworth, was among the survivors.

As usual in those dramatic days, there were tales of great courage and heroism. Like that of 18-years-old mess steward Jimmy Smith, who had left Heswall Nautical Training School in 1939 to join Canadian Pacific. Jimmy helped fight the blaze until told to abandon ship. But, with two other seamen, he made sure that an injured woman was put into a lifeboat.

Another unnamed steward climbed a rope up the scorching side of the burning liner and raced through flames to release a lifeboat, which probably saved another 40 lives. Because some of the lifeboats were burnt, the crew improvised rafts. The youngest passenger, baby Neville Hart, not then one year old, was tied in a blanket on the back of A/B J. McKever, who climbed down a swaying 60ft. rope to a lifeboat, where the baby's family was waiting.

And, how's this for a coincidence? . . . . Three Hoylake (Wirral) brothers named Trigg were among the Empress of Britain's crew. One of them, in a lifeboat, was picked up by a trawler in which another Trigg brother was serving!

An even greater coincidence, perhaps, which some would prefer to call poetic justice, followed a couple of days later, when U.32 was sunk by HMS Harvester and her officers and crew captured. A short time later, as prisoners of war, bound for a camp in Canada, the surviving crew of the U.32, except for Commander Jenisch, were put on board the Duchess of York — under the command of Captain Charles Sapsworth!

Empress of Britain III

The first liner to be built in a British shipyard (Fairfield's of Govan) with complete air-conditioning, Empress of Britain the third was also the first of twins ordered by Canadian Pacific. She continued the name given to her famous predecessor, bombed and torpedoed in 1942.

The orginal Empress of Britain, which made her maiden voyage from Liverpool to Quebec in May, 1906, and a sister to the ill-fated Empress of Ireland, was only 14,190 tons, but carried 1,487 passengers. She and the Empress of Ireland were the fastest ships on the North Atlantic for a time, beating their Allan Line rivals, the Victorian and the Virginian.

By the end of the Great War, Empress of Britain I had carried a million troops and evaded being sunk at least a dozen times. She was renamed Montroyal in April, 1924. In June, 1930, having led a very useful and active life, she was scrapped, and undoubtedly the largest "souvenir" to be taken or bought during the dismantling was her smoke room. This was incorporated into the Sola Strand Hotel, Stavanger.

Empress of Britain (I), renamed Montroyal, was one of the fastest ships on the North Atlantic. (Canadian Pacific)

To return, however, to the third Empress . . . . Her launching, as the company's first post-war passenger liner, on June 22, 1955, appropriately by the Queen, was preceded by another little historical episode. The Duke of Edinburgh missed his rendezvous with the Queen at Uddington Station, Lanarkshire, for this engagement, and others in Glasgow. A sudden change in weather conditions compelled the Duke's helicopter to land in a football field in West Lothian, about 20 miles from Edinburgh, instead of alighting alongside the Royal Train. Crowds lining the royal route through Glasgow were mystified when they saw the Queen being driven without the Duke. But, whisked off in a taxi, the Duke caught up with her as she was visiting a carpet factory.

"What happened to you?" smiled the Queen as he arrived. But the police, who had kept their radios hot with flying communications, had already told her that he was safe and on the way. Both were in good time for the launching, attended by an estimated crowd of 10,000, and Empress of Britain slid smoothly into the Clyde and dipped her bow as though in salute to the Queen.

Liverpool was a familiar port for the Empress's master, Captain Stanley W. Keay who, two years before he joined Canadian Pacific, in 1919, had been a cadet in the world-famous Merseyside training ship, Conway. He had obtained his master's certificate by the time he was 25. Captain Keay did not know that he had been appointed master of the Empress of Britain until a few weeks earlier when he had called at Liverpool in command of the Empress of France and, coincidentally, just as the Empress of Australia was leaving Liverpool for the Clyde where she was to be sold. This was a fitting command for the man who had been second and first officer, between 1935 and 1938, in the earlier Empress of Britain and was her navigating officer who was injured when she was sunk in 1940.

The 26,000-ton liner, every inch a traditional "White Empress" with a pepperpot funnel and the usual white hull and green boot topping, came to Liverpool on March 2, 1956. This was for underwater inspection in Gladstone Graving Dock, because no dry dock on Clydeside could accommodate her bulk. Still in the hands of her builders, she sailed again for the Clyde on March 8 and carried out her speed trials off the Isle of Arran. She returned to the Mersey early the next month to prepare for her maiden voyage from Liverpool to Quebec and Montreal on April 20.

But this "ladies' ship", as she was at first dubbed, was to make a late-heralded special-guest cruise before that . . . . She was known as the ladies' ship because intensive tests were carried out at Liverpool by blondes, brunettes and redheads, to discover the most flattering combination of decor and lighting to agree with their complexions! And because of the long and arduous hours of modelling within the various splendid sections of this luxurious vessel, for brochure and advertising purposes, not to mention posing for BBC Television cameras, this galaxy of lovelies were given free "tickets to ride". It happened like this . . . .

The special, pre-maiden voyage, or rather coastal trip, on April 9, was arranged to take selected guests from Liverpool to Southampton and give them a foretaste of the liner's luxuries during a 26-hour cruise. While those guests sped home from Southampton by Pullman coaches, another set of guests from the south returned with her to Liverpool. Four of the pretty Liverpool girls who had been modelling on board, were suddenly invited to sail to Southampton on this mini-cruise. It was a snap decision made by the company in recognition of the girls' good work. They were wildly excited, but how could they let their husbands and boy friends know at such short notice? Well, they did. Although the ship-to-shore telephone link was disconnected within minutes of the invitation, messages somehow were relayed, even by cablegram, and the girls sailed with the new Empress.

As I also sailed with the Empress of Britain on that passage, I can state with confidence that this was a smooth and entertaining cruise — entertaining in that we had on board the overseas "Twenty Questions" quiz team, with celebrities like Michael Miles, Anona Wynn .... and Canadian film star, Robert Beatty. Naturally, the questions (relayed to Canada) were all marine and maple-leaf slanted!

I claimed two minor "firsts" for Liverpool on that voyage, in being the first passenger to swim in Empress of Britain's lovely indoor pool, and by arranging for the first picture to be taken of a girl on the bridge of a brand-new, famous, £6,000,000 luxury liner. Captain Keay gave me permission for the photograph to be taken (by a Press Association cameraman) of the 18-years-old brunette — so long as she was accompanied by a qualified helmsman/AB at the wheel. That picture went round the world!

As Captain Keay told me, as we rounded the Lizard early that glorious sunny morning: "She behaves beautifully." (the Empress, of course!)

Empress of Britain's arrival at Southampton was a stirring occasion, for there, tied up at the Atlantic terminal to welcome her, was Cunard's dear old Queen Mary. The 80,000-ton Queen greeted the new Empress with three long stentorian blasts of her whistle, which must have been heard in Liverpool! And as she approached the terminal, the Empress was serenaded by some jolly music. A huge banner across the landing stage read: "Welcome and Good Luck Empress of Britain".

It is understandable that after this well-publicised trip, there was comparatively little fuss when she finally sailed from Liverpool on

Empress of Britain III ploughs a fine sweeping wake in a calm sea. Blondes, brunettes and redheads helped to decide the lighting in her public rooms!

her maiden voyage to Canada, although hundreds of goodwill messages and bouquets flowed on board. Perhaps, because of the early hour in which she left, no ships' sirens bade her bon-voyage, nor was she dressed overall.

Pacific Steam Navigation Company's brand-new liner, Reina del Mar, dressed overall, was in the river as she left. The latter was due to make her maiden voyage on May 3, but was then preparing to take special guests on a short cruise to the Western Isles of Scotland on April 20. The circumstances of these two new ships was almost a repeat of those in 1931 when Empress of Britain (II) arrived in the Mersey to prepare for her maiden voyage, and P.S.N.C.'s new luxury liner, Reina del Pacifico, was also in the port, ready to sail on her maiden voyage two days later!

Although she left Liverpool in relative quietude, the new Empress received a great welcome on the other side of the Herring Pond. Sirens galore, 500 spectators who had braved a drizzly day, and the music of the band of the Canadian Grenadier Guards, greeted her at Montreal, after that which her captain described as "a very nice trip", which took five days and 11 hours.

She bettered this time in her voyage from Montreal to Liverpool in July that year by breaking the post-war record for the Atlantic crossing between Father Point, Quebec, and the Bar Light at Liverpool in four days, 20 hours, 30 minutes, steaming 2,437 miles at an average speed of 20.9 knots. And she later improved on this.

New Year's Day, 1957, was a date that 500 Hungarian refugees will not forget, for that day they left Liverpool in the Empress of Britain to start a new life in Canada. For most of them, this was the biggest liner they had ever clapped eyes on.

By the end of that year she had replaced, on the Liverpool-Greenock-Montreal service, the Empress of Scotland, which made her last voyage as a C.P. liner on November 23, when she arrived at Liverpool from Montreal.

On October 9, 1959, Empress of Britain made news when she sailed from Liverpool to Canada with a BBC test aerial, via which, it was hoped, passengers would be able to watch television shows from both sides of the Atlantic.

Following a strike among some members of the National Union of Seamen on the liner in November, 1961, the union's general secretary, then Mr. Jim Scott, came to Liverpool to make what was probably an historical speech. The writing was on the wall for regular ocean travel and, as reported in the Liverpool Echo on November 5, 1961, when some 365 passengers were delayed, he asked his members:

"Will these people on board travel seaward again? I am going to suggest they will not because the time seems to have come when there is no guarantee that the passengers on the North Atlantic run, as a result of what is happening, will reach their destinations, and they are going to go by air. This has been evidenced right through the season. I am no friend of the shipowner. I want to extract as much from him as I can, and there is only one way I can do it and that is to see and ensure that he is getting passengers' rates and cargo freights." The Empress sailed, leaving 150 strikers behind.

As we have said, the writing was on the wall, and on December 31, the following year, Empress of Britain followed in the wake of her sister, Empress of England. She arrived at Liverpool on October 10, 1963, from her last voyage in the company's service and was leased to Max Wilson's new Travel Savings Association for full-time cruising.

In September, before starting her cruise the next month, Empress of Britain had made a 222-mile mercy dash to aid a seaman with a crushed hand on a Russian vessel. The liner, on her way from Canada to Liverpool, lowered a motor launch for her surgeon to attend the injured man on the trawler factory ship, Sovetskaja Rodina. The doctor's party returned .... with a packet of Russian cigarettes donated by the crew. For Canadian Pacific, this mercy errand must have cost several hundred pounds. But, as the company said: "No bill will be sent to the Russians. This will be put down to a service for the Brotherhood of the Sea."

Would that the milk of human kindness flowed so smoothly on land!

Sailors, in the main (and particularly in the Mersey!) are big-hearted lads and those in Empress of Britain were no exception. They not only "adopted" but also often treated youngsters at the Liverpool School for the Blind. Some of the children were even given a party, provided by the company, on board the liner.

Empress of Britain's great cruising enterprise was launched at Liverpool on October 25, 1963 when, dressed overall, festooned with streamers, carrying 900 passengers and serenaded by the pipes and drums of the Liverpool Scottish, she sailed for the sun south of Biscay. All the razzle-dazzle of a maiden voyage was there, including free champagne and wine for the passengers and sprays of flowers for the women in addition. With them went Mr. Max Wilson, the 36-years-old South African who formed Travel Savings Limited — cut-price cruises, saved for in advance. This was the parent company of Travel Savings Association, jointly owned by the Max Wilson Organisation and Canadian Pacific, Royal Mail and Union Castle, as equal partners.

A few weeks later, she was bound for South Africa, from where she was destined to make two cruises from Capetown to South America. And from Liverpool she carried 570 emigrants under the South African Government's assisted-emigration scheme. This was the largest single party to leave Britain for South Africa for many years. History had repeated itself, for it was from Liverpool, 120 years earlier, that 500 emigrants to South Africa had set out in three ships. They ate salt meat and hard-tack on that long voyage. The Empress of Britain provided eight-course dinners, with wine and music . . . .

But this liner was not to end her days cruising with the T.S.A. She went up for sale in February, 1964, because, in the words of

First of Canadian Pacific's post-war liners. Empress of Britain (III) proudly cleaves through a choppy sea. She was launched by Queen Elizabeth and later renamed by Queen Anne Marie of Greece.

Canadian Pacific, "the economics of passenger-operating are not what they should be." Cruise results had been disappointing and there had been reductions in the numbers of transatlantic passengers being carried. The contract with T.S.A. would terminate at the end of the year, when the liner would be open to offers.

It didn't take so long, however, to find a buyer, and the company announced at the end of February that the liner would be sold to the Greek Line for an undisclosed sum. Having completed her T.S.A. cruises, she returned to Liverpool on August 23, when permanent staff among her crew of 400 were absorbed into the company's other vessels.

Before she left Liverpool, Empress of Britain was renamed Queen Anna Maria. And thereby hangs a funny tale.

Three painters were summoned to paint the new name in Greek lettering on the liner's stern. But, because of a misunderstanding, Greek characters were painted on her bows as well, instead of, in English, according to accepted practice. It was a sharp-eyed Liverpool docker, homeward-bound in the dusk, who spotted the mistake. "That's a funny name on your ship!" he shouted to a Greek officer. The painters three were duly called back. And perched on a swinging platform by the light of silvery arc-lamps, they renamed the ship in English.

Queen Anna Maria left Liverpool for Genoa (whose Meriotti yard had won the contract to increase her tonnage by another 800 tons, with additional recreational facilities) on November 18, 1964. Under her Greek master, Captain John Polichroyiades, her new services would include voyages to New York, via Piraeus, Lisbon and Naples. And, because many Jewish passengers were expected to sail in her on voyages to Haifa, too, a synagogue on board was also planned.

She was not officially given her new name until four months later when, on March 14, Queen Anne Marie of Greece named her at Piraeus in the presence of King Constantine.

In spite of all the big plans, this liner was destined not to end her days in the service of the Greeks and she was laid up at Piraeus in January, 1975. She was sold the next year to the Carnival Cruise Line, of Miami, Florida, where she joined her old running mate of eleven years earlier, the ex-Empress of Canada, renamed Mardi Gras.

So, the Empress which became a queen, found herself with yet another name — Carnivale. A jolly name, if not so dignified. Although old "Empress" admirers were delighed to see the sisters together again, the reunion was a little sad. Their other post-war C.P. sister, Empress of England, which became Shaw Savill's uneconomic Ocean Monarch, had already made her last voyage some months earlier .... to the breaker's yard in Taiwan.

Empress of Canada (I)

One of Canadian Pacific's crack "Empresses", the Pacific Blue Riband holder, Empress of Canada, surprisingly was lured to her doom in the wartime Atlantic by a faked code message, resulting in great loss of life.

The 21,500-ton Empress spent most of her career in the Pacific, being the largest ship on that ocean for some time after making her maiden voyage from Falmouth to Hong Kong on May 5, 1922. She created a record in June, the following year, by sailing from Yokohama to Race Rocks, Vancouver Island, in 8 days, 10 hours, 53 minutes, at an average speed of 20.6 knots.

Empress of Canada returned to Britain in 1929 for overhaul and to be re-engined at Fairfield's who built her and launched her on the Clyde on August 17, 1920. She made a sea trial to Quebec in August, 1929, to establish a new transatlantic record of 5 days, 14 hours, 25 minutes. But in September, when on passage from Southampton to Vancouver, via New York, Panama and San Francisco, she ran on to rocks in foggy Juan de Fuca Straits. She was refloated and repaired. The Canada made her 199th and final Pacific crossing on September 2, 1939, the day before the official declaration of war with Germany.

Requisitioned in November, she eventually joined the "Multi-Million Dollar" Convoy — consisting of seven luxury liners — the others being the Queen Mary, Mauretania, Aquitania, Empress of Britain, Empress of Japan and the Andes. January, 1941, saw her carrying troops from Australia to Suez, and in August that year, with escorting warships, she took a Canadian contingent and a demolition partly to Spitzbergen under "Operation Gauntlet", then embarked 2,000 Russian evacuees for Archangel. Homeward bound from this engagement and transporting Free French troops and a British military mission, she called again at Spitzbergen, collected the demolition party and some 700 Norwegian evacuees, and returned to the Clyde.

Trooping to India and to North Africa, with nearly 2,000 souls on board, including 362 crew, 500 Italian prisoners of war and hundreds of Norwegian, Polish, French and Greek servicemen and refugees, she was torpedoed when 400 miles off Cape Palmas, at six minutes to midnight on March 13. The order to abandon ship was given fifteen minutes later, and a second torpedo struck her soon afterwards and she began sinking by the stern. The incident, in which 392 lives out of a total of 1,938 were lost, produced the amazing story that the Empress was actually "lured to her death".

Because of her speed and being able to outpace any U.boat, the liner travelled unescorted. On her eighth day out, her wireless operator received a coded message, instructing her to make for Takoradi instead of Freetown, where she had been bound for her

Empress of Canada (I), holder of the "Pacific Blue Riband", pictured against a rugged Canadian backdrop.   (Canadian Pacific)

first stop. One of the 300 Poles on board, who had volunteered to join the Royal Air Force in Britain, and who later became a British businessman, Mr. Jerry Panko said that he vividly remembered the liner's sudden change of course. "The ship wheeled round in a great semi-circle, traced in the sea by the wake of her propellers", he said.

Documents discovered in Germany after the war purported to show that the liner was deliberately brought into the path of a waiting submarine by this message, faked and coded in Berlin.

Some survivors said that the Italian submarine, Leonardo de Vinci, surfaced after her first torpedoes had hit the liner's starboard side. Her searchlight verified the Empress's name, and she then fired a second torpedo to finish her. Unable to board the crowded lifeboats and rafts, many of the victims were left in the shark-filled waters for some 12 hours. By the time the rescue ships arrived, hundreds were dead or missing.

Another story was that an Italian doctor, in charge of the prisoners in the liner, signalled to the submarine from an open porthole in his cabin, "homing" the sub on to the ship. Some of the Italian prisoners later confirmed that when the submarine surfaced, they yelled for help in Italian but were ignored and that the sub picked up only one survivor — the doctor.

A Merseyside man, Mr. J.W. Cheetham, of Irby, a member of the liner's crew at that time and in the ship's hospital lifeboat with 80 others, including the Italian doctor, declared that the latter flashed his torch at the U.boat, waving and shouting 'Viva il Duce!' "The Italian prisoners", he said, "were chased off the grablines of the submarine. All they wanted was the doctor, who definitely played a big part in the sinking of the Empress of Canada."

The Leonardo da Vinci's "glory" was shortlived. On May 23, 1943, when attacking another unarmed trooper off Spain, the British warships HMS Active and HMS Ness caught up with her, sinking her with all hands.

Another survivor, Mr. George A. Jones, of Mold, North Wales, who gave me his eye-witness account of the sinking, was night butcher with a Liverpool colleague, Jimmy Walker, on the Empress of Canada that grim night - Friday the Thirteenth. "We were in the bottom butcher's shop, directly over the boiler-room, and had just finished cleaning a load of turkeys" he said. "I had just said to Jimmy: 'How about a cuppa?' and had looked at my watch, showing 11.55, when we were hit. It was a terrific explosion, right under our feet, and the deck gave a heave."

George tried to close the watertight door leading to the boiler-room, when a great gust of steam and a smell of cordite burst through this. "At that time, the 8 to 12 watch was being relieved by the 12 to 4 watch, so both watches of engineers and boiler attendants must have been killed instantly," he said. "A few minutes later, the lights went out."

As though in a nightmare, George felt his way through the darkness to the boat-deck, which was crowded and confused with shouting in different languages. The boats on the starboard side of the ship could not be lowered because of the liner's heavy list. But all the port-side boats, which had been slung out, got away, some with women in them. A few life-rafts were also tossed over the side and other boats, secured to the deck, were freed to enable them to float when the ship went down.

When the second torpedo struck, George jumped 50 or 60 feet over the side into the dark water. There was no moon, he said. While swimming, he saw the submarine with its searchlight on and a lifeboat alongside it. "It was then that I heard a deep rumbling noise and realised it was the boilers going. It was a little lighter then, and I saw the poor Canada going down by the bow. Her stern came right up out of the water. I could make out some figures on the stern, and then she seemed to glide down into the water and was gone."

One of the men in the sea was about to be picked up, but the lifeboat went on to aid some drowning women. "Up to then, there had been no sharks or barracuda for the oil had kept them away,"

Dressed in her "White Empress" livery, Empress of Canada the first, pictured in Canada, her second home. (Canadian Pacific)

said George. "As the boat pulled away, the chap in the water shouted: 'If I don't make it, tell my Mam I was thinking about her.' I never found out who he was."

After some four hours in the sea, George managed to climb on to a raft and then, in the dawn, he saw another overloaded raft nearby. "There were six on this and one man in the water, hanging on. I shouted that I would try and come to them. I was maybe about 30 yards away when I heard an unearthly scream. A shark had got the chap who was in the water. The others had to let him go or the whole lot would have tipped over. After about half an hour. we managed to secure the two rafts together."

There were many rafts and boats dotted about among the wreckage, and as the sun was going down, a concerted effort was made to join them all together so that they would be seen more easily, in addition to bolstering the spirits of the occupants. George and his companions found an empty boat and climbed into it. They lived for nearly four days on a few malted-milk tablets and water, and felt terribly weary with hunger and constant rowing to prevent drifting. And they were blistered by the hot sun. Then help came. A Catalina flying-boat, which had spotted them on the day after the sinking, showed up again, followed later by three rescue ships — the destroyer Boreas and corvettes Petunia and Crocus.

Empress of Russia, which made her maiden voyage from Liverpool to the Far East on April 1, 1913. In peacetime, she sailed chiefly in the Pacific and became a valuable troop transport in both world wars. When sailing as a troopship between Puerto Rico and Newport News, Virginia, in 1941, the 17,000-ton Empress was short of firemen and volunteers were called for by the commanding officer. Among the passengers at that time was a young naval officer – Prince Philip of Greece (now the Duke of Edinburgh) – who readily did his stint as a trimmer! In October, 1943, the Empress and the Drottningholm carried 3,600 repatriated prisoners of war from Sweden to Leith. Empress of Russia was badly damaged by fire in September, 1945, while being reconditioned at Barrow for the repatriation of Canadian troops and their families. Two of her crew lost their lives and the liner finally was scrapped.

As the survivors, including the injured, were being hauled up the scrambling nets by the Navy, "the sharks", said George, "had become so bad that they tried to snap at us as we were climbing up. The sailors were issued with rifles to keep them off. The destroyer and one corvette dashed back to Freetown. We stayed another day, looking for stragglers but found no one and headed for Freetown. On the way, we buried 19 of those who had died from their injuries.

"As we had lost everything, we were given a tin of cigarettes from the Red Cross. Next day, we got a 30-shillings cash advance, out of which we had to pay five shillings for the cigarettes. Eventually, the Mauretania came to take us home. We were all looking forward to a month's survivors' leave, but on my fifth morning at home, I had a telegram to report to another ship. Our leave, apparently, had started the day the ship went down. That was the worse day I ever had."

George's new ship was the Empress of Scotland, and in this, a year later, on March 13, 1944, the chief steward, Mr. Parr (who had served in a similar capacity in the Empress of Canada) called his old shipmates to his room. "He told us that we were passing over the position where the Empress of Canada had sunk," said George. "He read a prayer and we drank to our absent friends. . . . . "

Britannic I, II & III

The Britannic was one of the last great Liverpool liners to disappear from Merseyside. She was also the last of the White Star Liners. Built by Harland and Wolff, here was a ship, broad, squat and powerful, and at 26,943 tons almost the twin of her sister, the 27,759-ton Georgic. She was launched on August 6, 1929, as the largest motor vessel in the world, and made her maiden voyage from Liverpool to New York, via Belfast and Glasgow, on June 28, 1930.

When owned by Cunard both the Britannic and the Georgic were permitted to retain their buff funnels (with black tops) and their White Star houseflag, which was flown above the Cunard flag.

Perhaps because the Britannic was one of the declining number of liners operating from Liverpool in the 1950's, or because she was recognised as a steady ship even in some of the worst storms, she was a great favourite on Merseyside in her latter years. Certainly the shipping reporters of Liverpool in those days had good reason to welcome her fortnightly sailings to New York, because the Cunard Company always laid on magnificent lunches for passengers on those dates — and the Press was invited, too!

The former White Star liner, Britannic (III), at Ocean Dock, Southampton, ready to make her first voyage from that port in April, 1935, to maintain a regular service with her sister, Georgic, on Cunard's London-Southampton-Havre-Queenstown-New York run.

Like all the Cunarders, Britannic was also famous for her wonderful food and some sumptuous meals were created by her chefs. Her artistic cold-buffet displays, resplendent with decorated whole salmon, meats of all kind, with elegant figures sculptured from solid blocks of ice, were so picturesque and appetising that it seemed sinful to mutilate them.

But all was not beer and skittles for newspapermen, with deadlines to meet. Famous passengers made news and the gatherers were on board to collect that news. So there wasn't really much opportunity for gorging on those was (sailing) days! Personally, I considered myself lucky if I managed to get halfway through a Henry IV steak, with Lincoln potato creamily mushrooming through its brown baked skin, before breaking away to track down a quarry in the labyrinth of cabined corridors and rooms.

As shipping reporters know, passenger-lists are most useful, but subjects of news do not necessarily oblige by sitting quietly in their cabins awaiting interviews. Boarding a liner on its arrival, for instance — generally early in the morning — one would often find that those folk being sought had had breakfast and vacated their cabins. They could be queuing for immigration procedure, or even on the point of disembarking. On departure, it was an even bet that the person whom one wished to interview would be late coming on board, and to find him or her before the liner's whistle blasts signalled "all visitors ashore" could involve a hurried, worried hunt.

Britannic, serving as a troopship, photographed at Capetown on November 25, 1940. (Cunard Archives)

I remember tracking down Viscount Montgomery's barrister brother from Canada on one such occasion. He wasn't in his cabin and I was lucky to recognise him among the hundreds of passengers on board — simply because he was the spitting image of Monty!

"Covering the waterfront" could be quite an ulcerish occupation, often involving uncivilised hours in bad weather, with snatched snacks of "char and wads" in dockside canteens, and tearing down gang-planks to find a working phone-booth.

Although, in the 'Fifties, passengers-in-a-hurry were chiefly looking skywards, the liners of Liverpool continued to bring in some interesting people who had the time to stand and stare and take the longer sea routes — holidays in themselves. Hundreds of internationally-renowned folk trod Britannic's decks, from politicians like Stanley Baldwin to film stars like Rita Hayworth (and the Aly Khan).

The liner carried a permanent celebrity in the late ex-boxer Dom Volante, the spritely Liverpool featherweight of the 'Thirties. A smart, trim figure, wearing white gloves, Dom would stand at the head of the gangway, welcoming passengers on board. Nominally a steward, Dom was also one of Britannic's gymnasium instructors, who sailed with the liner for ten years and regarded her as his second home.

Did Dom save the Coronation? . . . (see story).
Happy portrait of the late Liverpool boxer, Dom
Volante, pictured on board the Britannic, in which
he served as gym instructor.

The late Liverpool author and "Scouse" expert, Frank Shaw, related how Dom, in his boxing heyday, was travelling to New York in a Cunarder, accompained by his even more-famous boxer friend, Nel Tarleton. As the liner was leaving the landing stage, and Nelson was on deck waving goodbye to his well-wishers, Dom slipped below to their shared cabin. Their bedroom steward had unpacked Dom's one and only bag, and Dom immediately asked: "Whur's me clothes?" "In the closet, sir," said the steward, who, like many of those on the U.S. run, used American expressions. Dom could only think of one sort of closet-and spluttered: "What a place to put me clobber!"

Dom was said to have saved the Coronation of Queen Elizabeth from disaster ... he caught the Archbishop of Canterbury when His Grace fell from an exercise horse on board a month before the ceremony!

A non-smoker and non-drinker, Dom used to tell how film star Cesar Romero, as a passenger, would rise at 7 a.m. and run 12 times round the deck with him. And how Gracie Fields once sang ten songs to the crew. This, then, was Britannic III, and at this stage I would like to introduce her White Star predecessors. . . .

Britannic the first was a relatively small ship of only 500 tons, making her maiden voyage from Liverpool to New York on July 30, 1874. She seems to have led a fairly uneventful life, except for becoming a Boer War transport, and was scrapped in 1903.

The second Britannic, although not living long enough in the Great War to achieve the luxury-liner purpose for which she was built, has become more famous today (through the efforts of undersea-explorer Jacques Cousteau) than she was when she was sunk as a hospital ship. It happened like this. . . .

At 48,158 tons, she was one of White Star's three Belfast built, four-funnelled giants, her sisters being Titanic and Olympic. She lived for only 11 months and never had the chance to serve her company. Britannic II was launched in February, 1914, six months before World War 1, but was taken over by the Admiralty as a hospital ship in 1915, to join the Mauretania and the Aquitania in the Mediterranean to maintain a continuous hospital-ship service. This fine ship, orginally intended to convey hundreds of thousands of happy passengers between Britain and America in fabulously comfortable conditions, completed five trips to bring home a total of 15,000 wounded from the Dardenelles theatre of war.

She made her first and short-lived acquaintance with Liverpool on December 12, 1915, when handed over and commissioned. Thousands of Merseysiders turned out to see this huge vessel, the largest since the Olympic (45,324 tons), and described as aristocratic and better proportioned than either Olympic or Titanic. She made a

White Star Line's 5,000-ton liner, Britannic (I), built in 1874, pictured alongside Prince's Landing Stage, Liverpool. She made her maiden voyage from Liverpool to New York in August that year and, in 1887, was damaged in collision with the Celtic off Sandy Hook. She became a Boer War transport and was scrapped in 1903.

lovely picture on the Mersey, with her four buff funnels, hull and superstructure painted white, a 5ft-deep green band running her length 15 feet above the waterline and broken in three places on each side for huge red crosses. Two smaller red crosses hung from her boat-deck bulwarks and an illuminated red cross was hoisted between her first and second funnels at night, with 300 electric bulbs in each arm, and rows of green lights lit the boat-deck. Because she was so large and could not enter small harbours, Britannic II had to enlist the aid of shallow-draft craft, which carried the wounded out to her.

On her sixth and final voyage, in November, 1916, the Greece-bound Britannic was steaming through the Kea Channel from Naples after recoaling, to the Island of Lemnos, when there was an explosion. This was her death blow. The great ship shuddered and began to sink. There was no panic. Some of the 17 young Sea Scouts on board, in fact, continued to eat their breakfast.

Captain A.C. Bartlett, who was master of the tragic Titanic on her pre-maiden voyage from Belfast to Southampton, turned Britannic towards Zea Island in an attempt to run her ashore. But, in spite of the care that had been taken to ensure that Britannic's design and building specification were modified following the Titanic disaster, four a half years earlier, some 250 feet of the ship began to flood. Her propellers were still turning when her boats were being lowered and these caused most of the casualties. A total of 28 died, but the toll would have been far greater had she been on the return leg and consequently loaded with wounded.

The question whether Britannic was mined or torpedoed was argued for some sixty years. Popular opinion favoured a mine, although the Germans at the time declared: "The Britannic was transporting fresh troops for our enemies. If she had not been doing so, our submarines would never, of course, have torpedoed her." An Austrian, Adalbert Franz Messany, who had been transferred to the Britannic on October 31, 1916, presumably at Naples, charged that the ship was carrying 2,500 troops in her hold. This was denied by the British Government.

Fifteen Allied hospital ships were mined or torpedoed in World War 1 — nine confirmed as torpedoed. It took the skill of Captain Cousteau and his team on Calypso to confirm that Britannic was among those nine. In 1977, in a blaze of publicity which, except for the death toll, had an almost Titanic-like ring to it, Cousteau and his cameras found the old ship sixty years after she sank.

She was three miles from her chartered wreck position and 372 feet below the surface, with rusting beds, flattened funnels and other metals and slow-decaying debris forming the sea-floor pattern of her dying wake. Cousteau even filmed the tiles in Captain Barlett's shipboard bathroom. As the Titanic Commutator, the publication of the Titanic Historical Society, which covered this fascinating story in detail, proclaimed: "Contained within her shattered hull was a legacy of an era that would never live again. . ."

A rare picture of Britannic (II), built in 1915 by Harland and Wolff, Belfast. Designed to be the transatlantic sister of the Olympic and the Titanic, she and the Olympic were considerably modified and installed with many more lifeboats after the loss of the Titanic. Instead of becoming a luxury liner for the White Star Line, as originally intended, the 1914-18 war intervened and she was fitted out as a hospital ship. She first came to Liverpool on December 12, 1915, when she was commissioned. This giant vessel, at 48,000 tons the largest ship to be lost in the Great War, was sunk by a mine in the Aegean Sea on November 21, 1916, with the loss of 28 lives.

Passengers crowd the rails as Britannic leaves Liverpool in August, 1960, on one of her last voyages to America. (D.P. & E.)

The Britannic leaving Liverpool on November 11, 1960, on her last round trip to New York. She made 275 voyages in peace and in war, sailed 2,000,000 miles and carried 1,200,000 passengers before being scrapped, early in 1961.
(D.P. & E.)

The Britannic arriving in the Mersey on Sunday morning, December 4, 1960, with passengers from New York. After 32 years she was about to be scrapped. On the bow of this last of the White Star liners are the tug, Nelson, and the tender, Flying Breeze, dressed overall in honour of the final homecoming of the old favourite. (D.P. & E.)

Britannic's Christmas tree, destined never to celebrate Christmas . . . Head waiter Mr. Charles Leach pauses for thought in the liner's dining room on the day that she returned to Liverpool after her last passenger voyage.

* * *

So, Britannic No.3, last of the line, more than made up for her ill-fated predecessor. She had, in her 30 years' life, a few troubles. But then, few ships do not. She ran aground in Boston Harbour in December, 1933, and then, also in New England, in January, 1935, when the temperature fell to 40 degrees below zero, and she could not dock until tugs cut a lane in the ice for her. Fires presented her with more serious dangers and she survived quite a number of small outbreaks — even two in one day while in Huskisson Dock, Liverpool. The most serious fire was that which broke out in her hold when she was three days at sea, and 559 bags of mail were destroyed.

By 1960, Britannic's days were numbered, and she arrived at Liverpool on December 4, that year, from New York, on her last voyage from the States. She had completed 275 peacetime and wartime voyages, involving more than 2,000,000 miles and carrying over 1,200,000 passengers on Atlantic crossings and cruises. Although launched two years before her running mate, Georgic, the Britannic outlived her by five years.

When she sailed to the breaker's yard at Inverkeithing in January, 1961, she still proudly wore her White Star colours of buff and black.

Little of her remains, but the Merseyside Maritime Museum has custody of her forecastle bell and her huge, three-tone whistle, comprised of three bronze-alloy cylindrical bells and a three-branched copper steam pipe, which was mounted on Britannic's aft funnel. Another, of similar pattern, but air-operated, was fixed to the foremast. A tape of Britannic's "voice" — recorded by Mr. Harry Brookes, of Waterloo, before the liner left for the breaker's, is also with the museum.

Duchess of Bedford/Empress of France

Some ships seem to be lucky from the moment their keels are laid. The Duchess of Bedford , which became the Empress of France, was such a ship. During the last war, she sank a U.boat, damaged another, was shot at and bombed on a number of occasions, and once struck an iceberg without sustaining damage.

Launched on January 24, 1928, at John Brown's Clydeside yard, which produced many Canadian Pacific liners, the 20,123-ton Duchess of Bedford was one of the company's famous four "Duchesses", with sisters, Richmond, Atholl and York. All were detailed to Liverpool, often alternately sailing via Greenock, and the Bedford made her maiden voyage from Liverpool to Quebec and Montreal on June 1, 1928.

On May 8, 1933, she was the subject of an amazing rumour, which reported her sunk after striking an iceberg off Newfoundland. The misunderstanding of a message picked up by an unidentified wireless operator was thought to have been the cause of this story, which swept through the country. The distress this must have caused to relatives of those on board was not alleviated until 2 a.m. the following day, when the liner radioed from mid-ocean that all was well with her.

Arrival at Liverpool, in May, 1928, of the first of the famous Canadian Pacific "Duchess" ships – the new Duchess of Bedford, then the largest cabin-class steamship. (L.N.A.)

The Duchess of Bedford pictured in the Mersey in June, 1928, ready for her maiden voyage. Note the two starboard lifeboats by her foremast. (See story).
(Canadian Pacific)

But strange things happen at sea. Those who believe in premonitions might well have have nodded their heads sagely when, only two months later, on her July 13 voyage from Liverpool to Montreal, the Duchess of Bedford really did strike an iceberg in the foggy straits of Belle Isle, Newfoundland! Fortunately, she was undamaged.

Strange, too, that six years later, on June 9, 1939, she brought to Liverpool 32 French fishermen whom she had rescued from their sinking barquentine, Ben Hur, which had smashed into a monstrous (reported 130ft. high) iceberg off Newfoundland.

This incident was but a few short months from the outbreak of war and if all those who had sailed in the Duchess of Bedford during her comfortable and peaceful voyages in the mellow 'Thirties had found her a good ship, then surely, the thousands of troops she carried during her six years' wartime service must have felt equally secure within her. For, although called "the most bombed ship still afloat", not one of those she carried during those grim years was lost, and she came through it all virtually unscathed. As a troopship, she carried 179,000 servicemen and women and civilians, almost all over the world, and covered more than 400,000 miles.

Her luck was severely tested during the war. Requisitioned for trooping at the outset, she made her first voyage in this capacity to Bombay. Then, at Singapore in January, 1942, she took on board 875

evacuee women and children when the Japanese were already pouring into the city's streets. She was the last ship to leave the harbour before the island capitulated and managed to escape with little more than superficial damage. Although again attacked while on passage, she landed her passengers safely in Java before returning to Liverpool.

With a 6in. gun (made for the Great War nearly three decades earlier) mounted on her stern, the Duchess of Bedford, in August, 1942, sank a U.boat on a trip from Liverpool to Boston. She possibly damaged another U.boat, too.

The London Gazette, dated 22 December, 1942, recorded that, for the first action, the O.B.E. was awarded to Captain William George Busk-Wood, of Cosham, Hampshire; the M.B.E. to 4th Officer John Llewelyn Williams, of Prenton, Birkenhead, and the B.E.M. to the two stewards, Frank Fothergill, of Liverpool, and William John McCardle, of Bootle.

The citation read: "The master handled his ship with tactical skill when attacked by an enemy submarine. Fire was brought to bear under the direction of the fourth officer, the Oerlikon guns being served with coolness and accuracy by Fothergill and McCardle.

"The combined fire of the ships' guns destroyed the U-boat.

"Equally good work was done in an air attack four weeks later, when the enemy was driven off and the vessel saved from harm."

A fine study of the Empress of France (ex. Duchess of Bedford) as she heads out of the Mersey in February, 1956, on her first voyage after annual overhaul. (D.P. & E.)

Stewardess Mrs. Lilian O'Brien and chief bedroom steward Mr. Henry John Shannahan, preparing the private dining room in the Empress of France for Princess Elizabeth and Prince Philip. Sadly for them, the Royal couple, who toured Canada and visited the U.S., flew out to Canada and returned home in the Empress of Scotland. (D.P. & E.)

Mr. Williams told me that, to his knowledge, the Duchess of Bedford was the only troopship to sink a German U.boat by gunfire.

John was troopdeck officer at the time, in charge of the ship's defence. "We sighted the submarine in 53.54 North, 26.27 West, fine on the port bow," he said. "The Captain turned the ship around to put the submarine astern of us and we opened fire and hit the base of the conning tower with a 6-inch shell, as well as with Oerlikon fire, and she sank vertically by the stern."

Mr. Fothergill, who fired 75 rounds at the U.boat at point blank range, was said to have been avenged because he was torpedoed during the 1914-18 War!

The Duchess took part in three invasions — at North Africa. Anzio and Salerno. She carried American commandos to Salerno and was the headquarters ship there for a time. A prime target in this hot-spot, she survived heavy aerial bombardment and was credited with shooting down a torpedo-carrying bomber.

Even on her home doorstep, the Bedford was fair game to the enemy, but again she managed to avoid damage when a stick of bombs exploded close to her as she rode at anchor in the firelit, reflecting mirror of the Mersey during the Blitz of May, 1941.

The Duchess of Bedford sailed twice from Liverpool with thousands of repatriated Russian prisoners of war. On arrival at Odessa in 1945, her master, Captain H. Stuart Knight, was presented with a plaque by Commander Voronin, of the Soviety Navy, in charge of the repatriates. The gift was a token of appreciation for all that had been done for the Russians on the voyage and was later installed in the liner's main entrance.

An absorbing mystery concerned this liner when, as Duchess of Bedford, she was involved in a curious incident in 1942 or 1943, when steaming as a transport up the Red Sea towards Suez. This is a particularly hot and humid part of the world, with a scorching summertime climate, vast and arid deserts, and where the sea seems oily, or "painted" like that in The Ancient Mariner. And it's sheer hell to live below decks.

On her forward mast-house, known as the "for'ard island," she carried four lifeboats. These were positioned in pairs, one boat over the other, with a set of davits on each side of the island. Because it was wartime, when an emergency could arise in a flash, the upper boat was kept ready for launching — that is to say, slung out on its falls so

Empress of France in Gladstone Dock, Liverpool, showing the cowls fitted to her funnels, to prevent smoke pouring on to the open passenger decks.
(D.P. & E.)

Three White Empresses berthed together in Gladstone Dock, Bootle, in July, 1960, because of a seamen's strike. They are the Empress of France, Empress of England and the Empress of Britain (left). (D.P. & E.)

that the patent davits could be wound outboard. So when the starboard upper boat was found missing at dawn one day, rumours swept the ship. The davits had been wound out and the falls, lowered to the water, swung empty over the long bow wave.

On watch overnight, the story goes, there were two navigating officers, a quartermaster, a bridge messenger, and DEMS gunner (Defensively Equipped Merchant Ship), all of whom would have been in postion to notice any activity around those lifeboats. The deck crew also would have been in the area for much of the time. And, because of the heat, it would not be unusual for any number of the crew to come on deck for a breather in the cooler atmosphere.

How was that boat lowered and sailed away without, presumably, anyone seeing it? The technical difficulties of lowering the boat silently, getting it unhooked and away from the ship, probably steaming at 14 to 16 knots, seem almost insurmountable.

The story does not end here. Let me quote my informant, who later was connected with the ship, but was not sailing with her at the time:

"Two days later, a ship towed the missing lifeboat into Suez Bay and returned it to the Bedford. At this point, the officer commanding troops on board is said to have rushed down to the boat, taken a rifle from it and hurried back to the army staff room. (There was always a permanent army staff on board a troopship). It was rumoured that two non-commissioned officers were missing from the staff. . . . "

Loading in Gladstone Dock in October, 1960, before making her last voyage from Liverpool to Montreal. (D.P. & E.)

Top Right:
Mr. John Parkes, chief engineer, and Mr. Leslie McGowan, second engineer, on board the Empress of France, where the telegraph sadly signals "Finished with engines". (D.P. & E.)

Bottom Left:
Master of the Empress of France, Captain N.W. Duck bids farewell to his ship: "I like to think of her as retiring", he said. (D.P. & E.)

Intriguing story, isn't it? And wouldn't it be satisfying to know its sequel!

February, 1947, when most of the servicemen had been "demobbed", saw the Duchess of Bedford complete her last trooping voyage and she returned once more into the hands of the Scottish builders for a complete refit. She and the Duchess of Richmond became luxury liners once more, with most of their state-rooms rebuilt, and the company's house-flag insignia appeared on their funnels for the first time. Provisionally, she was renamed the Empress of India (III) but, meanwhile, as India had become a republic, she emerged as the Empress of France. With Empress of Canada, the only sister to survive the war with her, as the previous Duchess of Richmond, she rejoined the regular Liverpool-Quebec-Montreal service on September 1, 1948.

Fittingly, perhaps, for a lucky ship, Empress of France once carried from Liverpool to Canada, on part of its historic 50,000-mile journey round the world, the Cross of Jerusalem, in which, it is said,

Empress of France slips away quietly from Gladstone Dock, Bootle, in December, 1960, on her way to Avonmouth to be scrapped. Merseyside ships paid their tributes with mournful blasts on their sirens.   (D.P. & E.)

is inlaid a piece of the true Cross. She was also the ship originally chosen to take Princess Elizabeth and the Duke of Edinburgh to Canada on September 25, 1951, and preparations were started for the special furnishing of the royal suite on board. But, to the bitter disappointment of the captain, crew and undoubtedly the passengers who had booked for that voyage, the Royal passage was cancelled because of the King's illness, and the couple flew to Canada the following month. Canadian Pacific at least had the honour of providing a vessel for their return to Britain — the Empress of Scotland — which arrived at Liverpool on November 17 to a rousing Merseyside welcome.

Ships' lives generally being less than half man's "allotted span", the Bedford-cum-France did well to notch 32 full years of excellent service before she was finally sold for scrap after arriving at Liverpool from Montreal on December 7, 1960.

Georgic

A pre-war luxury liner of nearly 28,000 tons, the Georgic became one of Britain's greatest troopships — after she had become a bombed and burned-out shell at Suez in 1941. Britain's largest motor ship when built as White Star Line's last liner, she was a little bigger than the Britannic, two years her senior and almost her twin in appearance.

Both sisters had two squat, oval funnels (each of those forward were dummies), and slightly raked masts. Georgic differed from Britannic with a curved and streamlined bridge front.

White Star merged with Cunard in 1934, but these two ships always kept their distinctive White Star funnel colours in buff, with black tops, and flew that company's houseflag with the Cunard flag. Completed by Harland and Wolff in June, 1932, Georgic made her maiden voyage from Liverpool to New York in June 25 that year, as a running mate to the Britannic, and replacing the scrapped 21,000-ton Cedric.

On her first appearance in the Mersey, she was welcomed by Liverpool's Lord Mayor, Alderman J.C. Cross, who congratulated White Star on adding "such a wonderful jewel to the maritime crown of Liverpool". The B.B.C. installed 10 microphones in different parts of the liner for her special send-off broadcast, conducted by Victor Smythe.

The Georgic in wartime camouflage, as one of Britain's finest troopships. Note gun on stern.　　　　(Cunard archives, University of Liverpool)

Georgic's "Palm Court", pictured in 1932, the year she made her maiden voyage as a White Star passenger liner, and was described as "a wonderful jewel in the maritime crown of Liverpool".

"Dinkie", Georgic's cat, chose the maiden voyage as an auspicious occasion for producing three kittens, which some of the American passengers constructed as an excellent augury for the success of the new ship!

Thanks to their respective companies, the Liverpool liners made frequent contributions to charities, and over the years many socials and other functions were held on board the ships when they were in dock. The Georgic claimed the distinction of being the first liner to hold a ball at Liverpool. This was in aid of the British Legion and was held on October 19, 1932, when she lay in Gladstone Dock. Many of the guests, including some of the cast of the show, "White House Inn" at the city's Empire Theatre, had a swim in the liner's Pompeiian pool, and breakfast was served in the early hours, and later, to guests who had booked cabins and stayed the night.

Georgic made her first voyage from Southampton to New York on January 11, 1933, replacing the Olympic, which was on a long overhaul. While Georgic was at Southampton — from where she made two voyages to New York before going on a cruise — some 2,000 people visited her and the proceeds for this chargeable event went to local charities.

Between 1935 and 1939, the Georgic operated chiefly on the London-Havre-Southampton-New York Service, but came to Liverpool occasionally. She made five transatlantic trips in the early days of the war, although Americans had been told not to travel in her because she was a beligerent vessel.

Georgic's commercial work ceased in March, 1940, and she was prepared as a transport. That May, she helped evacuate British troops from Norway and, having brought them home, sailed once more to assist in the mass exodus from Brest and St. Nazaire. In spite of enduring heavy air attacks, she was not hit. She carried on trooping between the U.K. and the Middle East, America and Canada, and during the grim Battle of the Atlantic days, in February, 1941, sailed to New York to become the first British passenger liner to reach that port since the middle of the previous November. That voyage, however, was not without incident. She was saved from a U.boat attack by the Royal Air Force, which bombed and sank the prowling submarine.

Millions of folk throughout the world laughed at and loved that fine British actor, the late James Robertson Justice, renowned for his parts as a hospital consultant and, of course, as a ship's doctor, like his hilarious role in "Doctor At Sea". Few, however, knew that this

James Robertson Justice . . . "made a happy and settled ship's company."
(Courtesy of British Film Institute)

Sad chapter in the life of a great liner . . . Georgic bombed, burnt and beached at Suez in 1941, pictured before salvage operations.

distinguished actor really did go to sea before he became so famous in films and on stage. Mrs. Sheila Houghton, mother of maritime author Michael A. Houghton, of Merseyside, recalls meeting James, an officer in the Georgic, when serving as a nurse in QAIMNS (R) and being drafted to Egypt in May, 1941.

Joining the ship at Greenock, ready to sail via the Cape in convoy (date deferred, with the Bismarck on the prowl), she "was introduced to a flamboyant, hirsute figure with auburn beard, James Robertson Justice, then an engineer officer, and in his prime," she related in the magazine, 'Ships Monthly'. "He was to distinguish himself at voyage's end, and post-war, as a character actor. He was extremely amusing that afternoon and his wit and charming guffaw on the voyage made us a happy and settled ship's company. Another notable figure on board was the late Professor Ian Aird, FRCS, as a Medical Corps Major. In 1955, he pioneered the first Siamese Twins separation in surgery — Boko and Tomo — at the Hammersmith Hospital.

"Once sailed, the convoy soon passed Gibraltar and the Azores. There were occasional high-level aerial bombing runs and U.boat activity was felt near the African coast, but the convoy put in at Freetown, Ghana, safely, and, on passing the line, King Neptune appeared with a canvas tub on the foredeck. James Robertson Justice, with a crown and a trident, terrorised the first-timers with a salt-water farce he excelled at. When one complained of the rough

73

treatment he gave out, he bellowed: 'Do you want some more, Daughter of the Sea?"

"Durban was visited to pick up supplies and the Georgic sailed on to Aden with a small convoy. Once there, the ship moored at a buoy. Justice again amused everyone on board by diving off the fo'c'scle to join Arab boys diving off small boats and the tender to retrieve coins that were being thrown in. When he emerged from the shallows with a coin in his mouth, Justice shouted up: 'What about me, Madam?' he was an expert swimmer_and challenged anyone to race him in the ship's pool, in which he swam like a porpoise!

"Arriving at Suez on July 7, most of the ship's personnel bound for the desert war had disembarked. I and 30 others were put on a train at Suez for Ismailia and No.1 General Hospital. I heard that the Georgic was to take on many Italian internee women and children in the next few days, but, seven days later, she was bombed with incendiaries, which set her on fire . . . ."

Part of the fire-ravaged interior of the ship that was once a luxury liner.

Georgic's luck ran out that day, July 14. At Port Tewfik, she received direct hits from high explosives and incendiary bombs and caught fire. There were no troops on board and all but one of her crew were saved. After heroic efforts, her master, Captain A.C. Grieg, beached her, with 18 feet of water in her engine-room. It took two months' salvage work to refloat her and, on December 2, she was towed to Port Sudan and then Karachi by the Clan Campbell and the City of Sydney. She was then towed to Bombay for repairs. Overall, with the help of other ships, Georgic was towed 2,775 miles — probably the longest tow ever performed with a ship of her size.

Eventually, she managed to make it home to Liverpool, on March 1, 1943, at an average speed of 16 knots — and with a 5,000-ton cargo — to defeat the Nazis' earlier claims that she had been sunk with thousands of troops!

Harland and Wolff, of Belfast, her builders, took Georgic in hand and gave her a new look. Practically all her superstructure was rebuilt

Georgic finally made it back to Liverpool where she is seen here in March, 1943. With most of her superstructure rebuilt, she was back in service in 19 months as the "Super Trooper" (Cunard archives)

and, after 19 months, she returned to Liverpool as the "Super Trooper". Her fore funnel (a dummy, used as a radio-room and engineers' smoke-room) and her mainmast had been removed, and she returned to duty, carrying scores of thousands of service personnel, including repatriated prisoners of war from the Far East.

On Christmas day, 1945, flying the famous battle colours of the Fourteenth Army, she brought to Liverpool General Sir William Slim, former Commander-in-Chief, Allied Land Force, SEAC.

Thousands of service personnel were quarantined at Liverpool for some time when she arrived with a suspected smallpox victim in March, 1946. Troops on board the Duchess of Richmond, which had arrived from Bombay about the same time, with four smallpox cases, were in a similar plight, which culminated in mass vaccinations for 10,000 people. Ironically, Georgic's case turned out to be chicken-pox!

Georgic played a Jack-of-all-trades role in her career, and her swapped-about duties included being a trooper, migrant ship and transatlantic passenger liner, chartered by Cunard. Troops being transported to Korea in October, 1951, benefited from Georgic's lavish accommodation improvements, made for her temporary switch to liner de-luxe status especially to bring over American visitors to Britain for the Festival of Britain that year. She was also involved in two collisions. One, which resulted in a tug sinking in Durban Harbour, and the other with the cargo liner, Atreus, during a gale at Colombo.

After 23 years' excellent service, Georgic was put up for sale in April, 1955, but her days were not yet over. The decision was changed and she was made available for Australian migrant work. Unfortunately, she was not a happy ship during her latter days, which were marred by crew troubles. When 80 waiters walked off the ship in May, as she was about to sail with 1,800 emigrants, the passengers had to wait on at tables and wash dishes.

On the Georgic's return to Liverpool on November 20, 1955, Captain William Fitzgerald related a number of distressing events that occurred when on passage to Australia on her second emigrant voyage.

Two of her crew were caned at Capetown for assaulting a shipmate and more than thirty stewards walked off the ship when the two men were dismissed. At Port Melbourne, 30 crew members were fined for being drunk and disorderly. Captain Fitzgerald said that many of his crew were young, inexperienced men.

On the return leg of that voyage, the liner carried troops from Australia to Kuala Lumpur. She also picked up French Legionnaires, who had been fighting at Dien Bein Phu and who disembarked at Algiers.

That proved to be Georgic's last commercial voyage. The Ministry of Transport put her up for sale by tender and on December 11, she sailed to Scotland to be broken up.

Duchess of Richmond/Empress of Canada II

Sinking at sea in a storm, going down under the guns of an enemy, or even sailing to the breaker's yard after long and faithful service, are fates which one somehow expects of ships. So, the end of the fine liner Empress of Canada the second, by fire, in her home-based Liverpool dock, where she lay a burnt-out hulk for 14 months, was something of an anticlimax to her grand career spanning a quarter of a century. For 19 of those 25 years, she was known as the Duchess of Richmond, a 20,000-tonner by John Brown on the Clyde, and launched on June 18, 1928.

She made her maiden voyage from Liverpool on January 26, the following year, in the form of a six-week pleasure cruise to the Atlantic Islands and the west coast of Africa, returning on March 8. Among her passengers was the Chief Scout, Lt. General Sir Robert Baden-Powell, and Lady Powell. Later, in January, 1935, she was to carry the honeymooning Duke and Duchess of Kent on a cruise to the West Indies.

The first of her regular service runs from Liverpool to Canada was made on March 15, 1929, when she sailed to St.John, New Brunswick. She also experienced the first of her troubles then by

The Duchess of Richmond. She carried the Duke and Duchess of Kent on their honeymoon. (Canadian Pacific)

A fine silhouette of the Duchess of Richmond against the Cheshire bank of the Mersey on November 25, 1929, on her safe return from Montreal after a very stormy crossing. The Cunarder Laconia, from New York, which reached Liverpool the night before, had to miss calling at Queenstown because of the fierce weather. (D.P. & E.)

running aground in St.John's foggy harbour en route to Liverpool an April 28, when her passengers were transferred to the Montcalm. Also because of fog, she was involved in a slight collision with the 14,000-ton Cunarder, Alaunia, in the St. Lawerence on November 11, 1932, while at anchor.

But she was not so lucky about Christmastime, 1945, when involved in another collision at Gilbraltar and her bow was buckled. Some 748 passengers missed their Christmas in Britain as a result of her having to return to port for temporary repairs. The Duchess of Richmond sailed into another patch of excitement in April, 1937, when she broke from her moorings in Haifa harbour during a full gale. Her 1,000 English and Welsh passengers, pilgrims to the Holy Land, were compelled to prolong their stay ashore until the gale abated.

She was a troopship during the war and carried 31,000 civilians, 26,110 prisoners of war and more than 12,000 servicemen and women. In the invasion of North Africa, she was close to the P & O liner, Strathallan, when that ship was sunk by two torpedoes. March, 1945, saw her sailing to Odessa with 3,700 Russians who had been held prisoners in France. And she brought home 900 British servicemen — plus three stowaway women, two of whom were the Russian wives of soldiers on board, and the third, a Pole.

The Russians requested the ship to turn back for inspection when the women were found missing, but the liner sailed on.

Among her most important wartime cargoes were some British inventions, escorted by two professors who left Liverpool for the U.S.A. on August 30, 1940. This special assignment was an earnest of Britain's intention to share her knowledge with America.

Close-up of Canadian Pacific's house-flag insignia on the funnels of the Empress of Canada, pictured the day before she sailed on her first voyage (after reconversion from a troopship), on July 16, 1947. (D.P. & E.)

In the November of 1945, Duchess of Richmond brought from Rangoon to Liverpool the last of the remaining prisoners of war in Sumatra and Singapore. On her return from Bombay, in March, 1946, she was held in quarantine until four smallpox cases among service personnel on board were removed into isolation. Coincidentally, the Georgic had also arrived at Liverpool with servicemen, including a smallpox case. The incidents resulted in nearly 10,000 people being involved in the largest mass-vaccination of passengers and crews ever undertaken in the port of Liverpool.

Duchess of Richmond in her new guise as the Empress of Canada, outward-bound from the Mersey. (Canadian Pacific)

Overhauled and refurbished in the winter of 1946-47 for her peacetime role, the liner was renamed Empress of Canada and she made her first voyage under this name on July 16, 1947, from Liverpool to Montreal under the command of Captain E.A. Shergold, who became Canadian Pacific Steamship's general manager in 1952. Liverpool gave her a great welcome on her return from this round-trip and among her passengers was the city's and the country's greatest current comedian, Tommy Handley, of I.T.M.A. (It's That Man Again) radio fame. Said Tommy, when he met the Lord Mayor of Liverpool (Alderman W.G. Gregson) on the promenade deck: "Well, if it isn't the chief of the Scousers!"

During the tugmen's strike, on April 21, 1948, Empress of Canada was controlled in one of the finest feats of seamanship seen in the Mersey for many years, when she moved from her berth in Gladstone Dock through the lock and up river to Prince's Landing Stage without the aid of tugs.

After a "lovely crossing" from Canada, the Empress went into Gladstone Dock again on January 10, 1953, for her annual overhaul. She was due to return to service on February 11. But this was a date she was unable to keep. . . . On Sunday, January 25, in the wet dock, she caught fire and, in spite of tremendous efforts by firemen from all over the north west of England, eventually she slid on to her side and became a burned-out totally-lost ship. Coincidentally, this took place only two months after Canadian Pacific had ordered a new 22,500-ton liner from Clydeside to replace one of their Empresses.

In Europe's biggest ship salvage operation, involving numerous engineers, divers and workmen in 14 months' heavy toil, the cutting away of hundreds of tons of entangled and broken superstructure, she was righted by winches, hawsers and pontoons, raised, patched and refloated in March, 1954, at a cost of some half-million pounds. Finally, on September 1, that year, she was towed out of Liverpool for the last time — to her Italian grave in the breakers' yard at Spezia.

Empress of Canada (II), as she will be remembered . . . at Prince's Landing Stage, Liverpool, before the disastrous fire. (Canadian Pacific)

These sensational pictures, shown on the following pages, taken by the Liverpool Daily Post and Echo, show the grim finale to the career of the Empress of Canada, a well-loved liner. She caught fire in Gladstone Dock, Bootle, on January 25, 1953, when undergoing her annual (Coronation Year) overhaul . . .

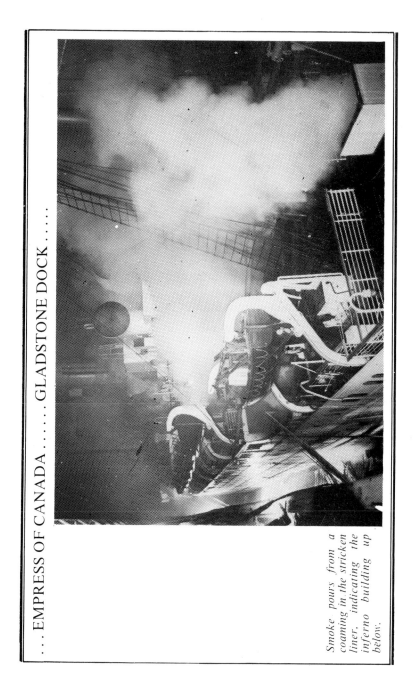

Smoke pours from a coaming in the stricken liner, indicating the inferno building up below.

...EMPRESS OF CANADA...... GLADSTONE DOCK......

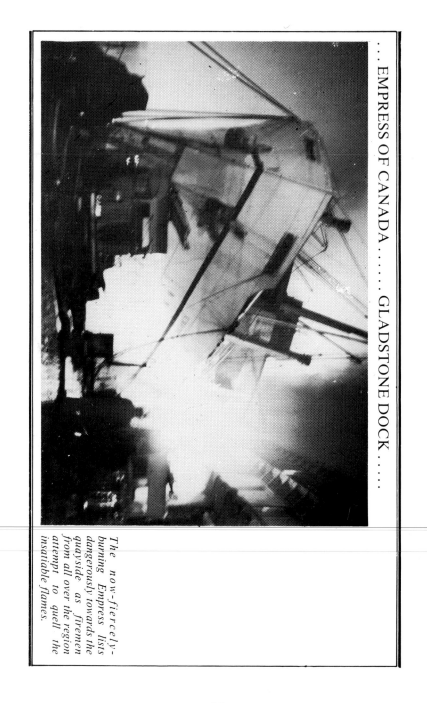

The now-fiercely-burning Empress lists dangerously towards the quayside as firemen from all over the region attempt to quell the insatiable flames.

Although well alight, the Empress still shows an unscorched upper stern in this picture, taken from the deck of her sister, the Empress of France:

. . . EMPRESS OF CANADA . . . . . . GLADSTONE DOCK . . . . . .

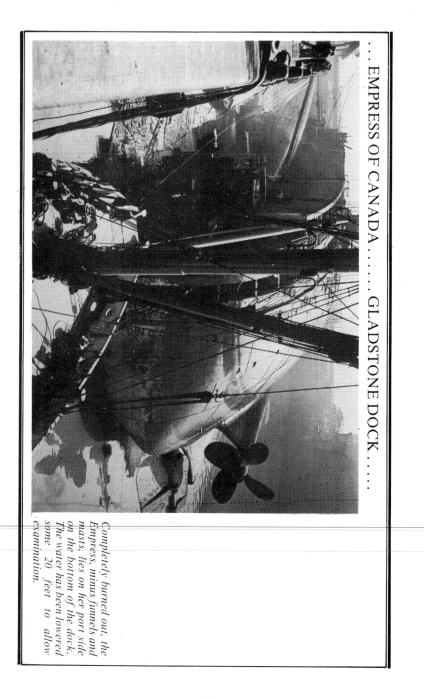

Completely burned out, the Empress, minus funnels and masts, lies on her port side on the bottom of the dock. The water has been lowered some 20 feet to allow examination.

Raising the giant liner begins . . . 9-inch hawsers, each exerting 110 tons pull from the winches and, attached to steel tripods fastened to the liner's side, take the strain.

... EMPRESS OF CANADA ...... GLADSTONE DOCK ......

Sixteen steam winches were used in the successful operation to right the fire damaged liner. Steam was provided by a boiler ashore and dredgers moored at the dock quayside.

... EMPRESS OF CANADA ...... GLADSTONE DOCK .....

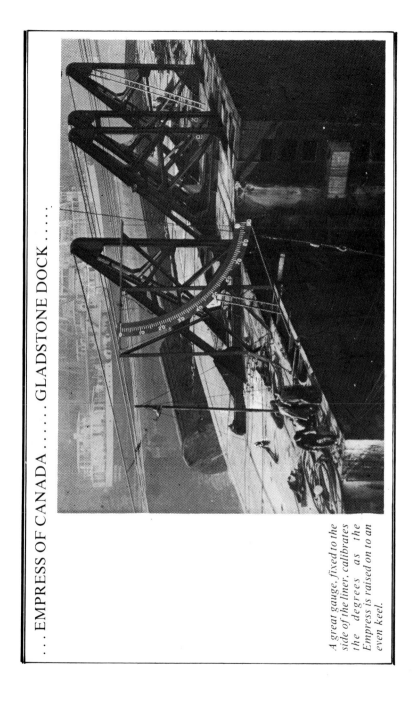

A great gauge, fixed to the side of the liner, calibrates the degrees as the Empress is raised on to an even keel.

EMPRESS OF CANADA . . . . GLADSTONE DOCK . . . . . .

A blackened ghost of her glorious prime, Empress of Canada undergoes graving-dock repairs to make her seaworthy for her last voyage.

... EMPRESS OF CANADA ...... GLADSTONE DOCK......

The hulk of the Empress being manoeuvred by the tugs' Wallasey and Salthouse, in Gladstone, Basin, Bootle, in September, 1954, in preparation for her towing by Dutch deep-sea tugs, to the breaker's yard at Spezia, Italy.

EMPRESS OF CANADA . . . . . . GLADSTONE DOCK . . . . . .

An 18-day inquiry into the disaster was held by the Ministry of Transport. Pictured, centre, is Mr. K.S. Carpmael, Q.C. (Commissioner of Wrecks), who conducted this, with four assessors – left to right, Mr. I.J. Gray, Captain L. Parfitt, Mr. W.J. Nutton and Mr. F. Dann. A lit cigarette-end was thought to have been the probable cause of the fire.

Empress of Canada III

Last of the line of the famous "White Empresses", Canadian Pacific's 25,600-ton Empress of Canada (the third) spent 10 years of her life based at Liverpool. The successor to the liner which burnt out in Gladstone Dock, she was built by Vickers Armstrong at Walker-on-Tyne and made her maiden voyage from Liverpool to Montreal on April 24th, 1961, under the command of Captain J.P. Dobson.

When the sailing programme for both the Empress of Canada and her sister, Empress of England, was announced, with heavy bookings, in 1965, Merseyside welcomed the news. It seemed as if there had been a general change of heart among travellers and that folk once again were looking to the luxurious, leisurely way of crossing the Atlantic, and also to cruising. There were even suggestions that Liverpool should build a proper waterfront terminal to receive overseas visitors. Those dreams, however, were short-lived, even though Canadian Pacific did successfully improve their liners' turn-round times by eliminating their movements into Gladstone Dock between sailings.

Empress of Canada was involved in what must be a unique experience for a ship. In April, 1967, she rammed a large whale when on passage to Liverpool from Canada, and her bow became embedded in the creature. She was put astern and eventually the whale was shaken off. Then she was delayed considerably longer when she ran into a near-hurricane and had to heave-to for eight hours to ride this out.

Such is the camaraderie among men (and children in this instance) who go down to the sea in ships, that it is not below the dignity of the captain of an ocean liner to stop for a tiny dinghy in distress. This is what happened in August, 1967, when two young boys, sailing in the Clyde, got into difficulties and were fortunately spotted by the incoming Empress of Canada's master, Captain Richard Walgate. He stopped the liner and had a lifeboat lowered to pick up the children. Their dinghy was taken in tow.

The first chill wind indicating the possibility that the Empress of Canada and the Empress of England might be sold, blew in May, 1968. But this was denied by the company, which forecast an upswing in the market, that it largely had to itself.

Thousands of emigrants and visitors to Canada continued to use these fine ships, as did huge numbers of those from the other side of the Atlantic, whose first footings on their European holidays were at Liverpool. With personalities, including royalty, among her passengers, Empress of Canada was constantly in the news. And so were the many "ordinary" passengers who had, perhaps, saved like

Successor to the liner which made maritime salvage history when raised from a Liverpool dock after she was burned out, Empress of Canada (III) was the last of the 80-year-old line of "White Empresses". After 10 years operating out of Liverpool she docked there for the last time on November 23, 1971, and later became a Miami-based cruise ship. (Canadian Pacific)

mad for years simply to visit their loved ones overseas. And the wealthy, too, like the ageing Mr. Charlie Farner and his wife, Leatha, who always declared themselves as having "no fixed abode" — because they spent their lives travelling all over the world! There were passengers like the late popular writer, Godfrey Winn, who, in the autumn of 1968, fulfilled the ambition he had cherished since he was a boy standing on Liverpool landing stage watching the ships go by — to sail across the Atlantic, first-class in a luxury liner.

Empress of Canada had her troubles. In January, 1970, for example, 400 of her 500 crew threatened to refuse to sail her out of New York on a cruise. They protested that inadequate arrangements had been made to fly them home to Liverpool, where most of them lived, during the six months the ship was based in New York. She finally sailed under a new master.

Hard in the wake of this disturbance came the news, on January 20, that the 25,000-ton Empress of England was to be withdrawn from service the following April — beaten by drastic cuts in air fares and the introduction of the Jumbo jets. Empress of Canada was then scheduled to operate the North Atlantic passenger service to Montreal, and the winter Caribbean cruises, with no partner to share these duties. She continued to benefit from the withdrawal and subsequent sale of the Empress of England and, said Canadian Pacific: ".... there is no reason why we should not operate on a viable basis for many years to come. We are extremely optimistic about the future."

94

Part of the sedate Carleton restaurant in Empress of Canada III.

(Canadian Pacific)

As the only major liner operating from Liverpool, Empress of Canada, in November, 1970, was suddenly switched to Southampton, from where she left for her winter cruises. The following January, Canadian Pacific warned of finding another port for her. It was worried over the future of passenger-ship handling on the Mersey after the threatened closure of the landing stage.

July brought company denials that the Empress was up for sale for 8,000,000 dollars, and she continued to sail from Liverpool. Then, on November 9, the company confirmed that it was withdrawing her from transatlantic and cruise services from November 23, when she returned to Liverpool. This was a heavy blow to her 500 crew, who faced coming ashore to join hundreds of other redundant seamen.

Three big ships at the Liverpool landing stage – as late as May, 1970. Empress of Canada (III) is seen in the centre, with H.M.S. Albion, the visiting aircraft carrier, to the left, and the Manx Maid, Isle of Man ferry, on the right.
(Bob Bird, Wallasey)

Still a comparative youngster of ten, Empress of Canada sailed from the Mersey for the last time on December 14, 1971, bound for Tilbury to await sale. And a piece of Liverpool's heart went with her.

Bought up by the American company, Carnival Cruise Line, she was renamed Mardi Gras and was later rejoined by her former running mate, Empress of Britain, which had been operating for the Greek Line and was renamed Carnivale. The pair sailed on weekly cruises out of Miami. Ironically, the other vessel of C.P.'s post-war fleet, Empress of England, which became Shaw Savill's Ocean Monarch, never joined her sisters. As you will read in the next chapter, she was broken up at Taiwan in 1975.

Empress of England

In spite of the number of "Empress" ships built by Canadian Pacific since 1891, it was not until May 9, 1956, that an Empress of England was launched. Up to then, there had been three Empresses of Britain, an Empress of Ireland and of Scotland (but no Empress of Wales), and Empresses of many other countries.

Lady Eden, wife of the world-famous statesman and one-time British Foreign Secretary, Sir Anthony Eden, did the honours by naming the liner at her Tyneside launching as sister ship to the last Empress of Britain, launched by the Queen the previous summer.

Built by Vickers Armstrong's, at Walker-on-Tyne, she was 25,000 tons and it was cheering and reassuring to hear that she was to be used to provide a more frequent Liverpool-Montreal service, starting with her maiden voyage on April 18, 1957. She was the subject of the BBC Television documentary "Tomorrow She Sails", on the eve of her departure for Canada. One of the cameras for this was operated from the top of Mammoth, the biggest floating crane in Britain.

Captain Charles L.de Hàuteville Bell, an Old Conway and a native of Formby, Lancashire, and formerly master of the Empress of Scotland, took comand of the Empress of England. He had been with Canadian Pacific since 1918 and was awarded the DSC for the last-war action against submarines while in command of HMS Whitehall. As the liner arrived at Prince's Landing Stage from Gladstone Dock, dressed overall for her maiden voyage, Captain Bell remembered Lady Eden, who had named his ship. He sent a cable of greetings from himself, the ship's company and passengers, conveying to her then sick husband their best wishes for his restoration to good health.

Empress of England was fortunate to have sailed on time. She left the builder's yard only an hour after a strike began there. She had accommodation for 1,058 passengers (158 first-class and 900 tourist) and, like the Empress of Britain, she was completely air-conditioned. Her average speed was 20 knots; she was fitted with stabilisers to reduce roll, and a "fireman's helmet" funnel to keep all smoke from her decks, irrespective of wind-force or direction. Other features of this noble ship were her sun and garden lounge, drawing room, clubroom, library, children's playroom, restaurant, cinema and Empress Room.

"A magnificent ship, a memorable voyage," said Captain Bell on arrival to a huge welcome at Montreal.

Almost exactly two years after this maiden voyage, Empress of England answered a mid-Atlantic S.O.S. from the German freighter Sonderburg, and picked up a sick American tourist who was on board. Passengers crowded the liner's rails as she hove-to in a heavy

Empress of England entering Gladstone Dock, Bootle, after her trials. She made her maiden voyage from Liverpool to Canada on April 18, 1957.

swell while the sick man was rowed across to her in a boat from the freighter.

Like a number of the Liverpool liners; her schedule was upset during the unofficial seamen's strike in July, 1960, and she missed a voyage when half her deck and engineering crew walked off three hours before sailing time.

Canadian and British police investigated mysterious small fires which broke out in five cabins in the liner shortly before she left Montreal for Liverpool in September, 1961. Arson was suspected.

The following January saw Empress of England sailing on the company's first cruise from Liverpool for many years. She made a 17-day cruise, including calls at Tenerife, Las Palmas, Casablanca, Tangier and Lisbon.

In a severe gale (which killed two people in Liverpool) in December, 1962, the Empress was damaged while in Gladstone Dock. She swung round on her bow mooring, having ripped a bollard out of the quayside. As she drifted across the dock, her sirens blaring a warning, two tugs went to her assistance and her stern anchor was dropped. But she struck a concrete knuckle, which caused a 20ft. gash in her side and her stern crushed up against the 9,000-ton freighter Hindustan. Although no damage was caused to the latter, the liner blocked the dock for about 12 hours.

On charter to Max Wilson's Travel Savings Association, and with her regular crew boosted by a party of attractive young hostesses, Empress of England made her first trip south of the equator in

November, 1963. A band played her out of foggy Liverpool on November 28, as she sailed away for 4½ months of tropical cruising — first to Capetown and then on three-week cruises between Durban and South America, with one to the Seychelles. She went cruising again in the winter of 1964-65 .... five luxury, one-class cruises, including the Atlantic Isles and the West Indies.

What happens to Christmas when a British liner leaves the frost and snow of wintertime Britain for the tropical sunshine? I can assure you, it is still celebrated in all its English tradition — mountains of food, plum-pud and cake and all, the whole gamut of drinks, trees, holly, decorations, crackers and so on. And so what if the Empress of England was south of Biscay on December 25, 1964? Ubiquitous Santa Clause simply came on board at Madeira to hand out his goodies to the youngsters. At least, Santa would find the Empress's "chimneys" roomy enough!

But is the traditional, heavy British Christmas fare appreciated on a tropical trip? Well, listen to what Mr. Charles Fulcher, former chief catering superintendent of Canadian Pacific once had to say about this ..... "Our ships are all air-conditioned, so down in the restaurants the temperature is always pretty even — and an Englishman likes a traditional Christmas dinner, whether he eats it on the beach at Honolulu or back at home!"

Sailors, of course, can expect to be at sea at Christmastime — it nearly always seems to work that way, they'll tell you. Mr. Owen Jones, of Rhuddlan, North Wales, for example, who was in charge of the Empress of England's catering department when the liner made her Christmas cruise in 1965, said he had spent only three Christmases at home in his 40 years at sea.

Having savoured a number of strikes in her relatively young life, Empress of England made more British maritime history in July, 1965, when she became the first ship operating from a British port to carry seamen's shop stewards and a convenor on board. Naturally, the National Union of Seamen was delighted with this move, the outcome of talks with the company. "A new page in maritime history", enthused a union official . . . .

On November 8, that year, the liner was in collision with the 12,369-ton Norwegian tanker Lifjord in the St. Lawrence Seaway, as both ships were leaving Quebec for Montreal. The Empress's bows were holed, her stern damaged, and she had to put into Quebec for temporary repairs. This incident revived memories of the far more tragic collision between the old Empress of Ireland and the 3,561-ton Norwegian collier Storstad, in the foggy Gulf of St. Lawrence on May 28, 1914.

But there was not much wrong with this liner's bows when, in February, 1966, she rode out a hurricane off the North Africa coast.

She was on a 16-day cruise with passengers including the British actor Raymond Francis (Det. Chief Lockhart of television's "No Hiding Place") and "opposition" scriptwriter, David Ellis, of "Dixon of Dock Green" fame.

"Running away to sea" has been almost commonplace for centuries among the youth of our island home. Some make it, and some don't — like the Lancashire approved-schoolboy, who tried to stow away on the Empress of England when she was due to sail on her sunny Atlantic Islands cruise out of Liverpool in March, 1967. The lad was discovered just after the ship left Liverpool. Although ignominiously handed over to the police via the Amlwych pilot boat in Moelfre Bay at nearly midnight off gale-swept Anglesey, he no doubt still boasts how he once stopped an ocean liner on passage.

September, 1967, saw "Ocean Travel Fortnight" when the public was admitted to certain liners at Liverpool. These occasions were very popular pre-war but the revival of such gestures seemed but a brave show in a climate fast cooling for liner passenger traffic. Only a few days earlier, there were straws in the winds when Canadian Pacific announced that, with Empress of Canada and Empress of England, it would be the only shipping line providing regular passenger services to North America from Liverpool and the Clyde the following year . . . .

When the liner arrived in the Clyde from Canada on November 13, 1968, shortly before sailing for Liverpool on the last leg of her voyage, she was breaking a 40-year link between Canadian Pacific and the Clyde. It was a sad occasion as she left, with pipers playing laments and, of course, "Will Ye No Come Back Again?"

But there's always the exception to the rule, and as illness takes a high priority, Empress of England found herself back in Greenock in September, 1969, on passage from Montreal to Liverpool, to land a sick crew member. Captain William Williams had radioed in advance for medical help and diverted the liner at full speed to put 16-years-old laundry boy, George Hazzard, ashore. George, making his first voyage, was simply unlucky. He fell down a companion-way.

A spot of equine history will always be linked with the Empress of England in that she was the first passenger liner to permit a pony to pace her deck like a passenger. Certainly, the pony was the first to travel on a C.P. ship, and it happened like this ... The pony, "Buttons", was virtually one of the family of Dr. and Mrs. Archie McPhail, who decided to emigrate to Ontario from Sandwich, Kent. And their 10-years-old daughter, Fiona, who rode Buttons, made her decision, too. "Buttons also goes to Canada, or I'm not going!" said she. Fiona had her way. A £50 passage was booked for Buttons, the first passenger to embark, and Fiona arrived to give him an airing on the deck.

Empress of England in her new livery, at Prince's Landing Stage, Liverpool, on December 20, 1968, ready to embark passengers for a Christmas cruise. Her familiar red and white chequered funnel design has gone and "C.P. Ships" is now emblazoned on her sides. (Canadian Pacific)

The liner's appearance changed that year. She arrived at Prince's Landing Stage on December 20 to embark passengers for her Christmas "islands in the sun" cruise, with the huge "C.P. Ships" painted on her sides. Gone, too, were the traditional red and white squares on her funnel, However, her new look was to be short-lived.

News of the "abdication" of the Empress of England, in January, 1970, hit Merseyside like a bomb. Announcing its decision to sell the liner, which was being withdrawn on April 1, the company made this laconic statement:

"The decision to withdraw the passenger liner from service and put her up for sale was made on the basis of 1969 operating costs and the forecast for 1970. Withdrawal of the Empress of England from service will permit Canadian Pacific to concentrate its full marketing and promotional efforts on achieving a high level of bookings for its remaining passenger liner, the more modern Empress of Canada. With increasing air travel and the prospect of even lower air fares, it is uneconomical to continue operating two passenger liners on the Atlantic."

Apparently, the loss projected in 1970 was several million dollars. And so there was one!

Empress of England was on a cruise, somewhere near Rio de Janeiro when that news broke, and when the liner docked at Liverpool on March 31, Captain Williams said he felt that "we have maintained a very high standard right to the end . . . . nostalgic, but not a sad occasion", he declared.

Sad enough, however, one suspects, for the 500-strong crew, not all of whom could be integrated into the remaining liner. As the National Union of Seamen pointed out at the time, Britain's passenger ships had been reduced from 509 before the war, with a total deadweight tonnage of 2,959,000 to 213 in 1964, with a total tonnage of 1,268,000, and a mere 135 in the autumn of 1969, with a slightly raised tonnage.

Shaw Savill Line bought the Empress of England on April 3 for an undisclosed sum, with the intention of converting her into a single-class liner to augment their round-the-world service and cruise ships, the Southern Cross and the Northern Star. Still regally dignified under her new name of Ocean Monarch, the liner sailed from Liverpool to Australia on April 11, 1970, on her first voyage for her new owners. She called at Las Palmas, Capetown, Durban, Freemantle, Adelaide and Sydney, and made a series of Pacific cruises, including a 38-day cruise to Japan for EXPO '70 visitors.

The seven-month £2 million contract to refit the liner at Cammell Laird's, Birkenhead, from September, was welcomed on Merseyside. Ocean Monarch was still based at Liverpool and, as the saying goes, "a rose by any other name would smell as sweet!" Unavoidable refit delay, however, caused Shaw Savill to cancel seven of its eight planned cruises for 1971. It cost Cammell Laird's an estimated £1,250,000 loss for the year because of "a serious miscalculation" of the cost of refitting Ocean Monarch.

This was an all-round financial disaster because it also cost Shaw Savill amost its entire summer cruising programme, which would have amounted to about £12,000,000 in revenue. The state of the parties can be visualised with the liner becoming the first-ever cruise ship to sail out of the oil-tanker cleaning berth at Tranmere, Birkenhead, on passage to Southampton, with a shipyard workforce still on board to finish off the job they began a year earlier!

Her arrival at Southampton, however, for another trip to the Atlantic Isles, swung her back into the glamour spotlight in which the general public usually views luxury ocean liners. And 70 attractive girls went on board to lend even more glamour and charm to the occasion. These were the new waitresses, smartly attired in navy-blue and white uniforms, who had been chosen from 1,200 applicants to brighten up the liner's mealtimes. Good service, laced with charm, would no doubt return a healthy glow to the pallid cheeks of sea-sick passengers!

But ships, even such as these, as I have said earlier, are not always so comfortable beyond those limits reserved for their passengers, and dissent among crews at sea has never been uncommon. Still, it must have been a traumatic occasion when more than 200 seamen and women crew members in dispute walked off the ship at Sydney during her world cruise in January, 1973. Some returned to the ship and completed the voyage, but the company chartered aircraft to fly 191 dissentients back to Britain.

An indication that Ocean Monarch's life expectancy was on a rapid countdown came in September, the next year, when she was compelled to return to Southampton with 800 cruise passengers because of engine troubles. Sure enough, her sale to a breaker's yard in Taiwan was announced and there she sailed on June 13, 1975. A virtual youngster of 18, she had been born too late. The heyday of the liners was over. She was just a white-hulled elephant . . . .

Ceramic

Ceramic was known as "The Relief of Bootle" because she employed so many of that Merseyside town's seafarers and consequently helped prune its dole and public assistance queues.

But there are still many folk thereabouts today who would rather have seen their relatives "cap-in-hand" than serving with the Ceramic on that dreadful wartime winter night of December 6, 1942, when she was torpedoed in the cold, gale-swept Atlantic with the loss of all her 278 crew and 378 passengers . . . but one.

Mr. Eric Munday, now a surveyor, living in Surrey, is that sole survivor, whose incredible story I shall relate.

Ceramic was sunk almost exactly 30 years from the date of her Belfast launching for the White Star Line, on 11 December, 1912. Ironically, she had survived the 1914-18 War as a commercial ship and a troopship, in spite of two U. boat attacks on her. She made her maiden voyage from Liverpool to Sydney, via the Cape, on July 24, 1913, and continued on that service until 1934, when White Star sold its interests and vessels to the Shaw Savill Line. A three-screw vessel of 18,750 tons, remodernised in 1936, she was the largest ship trading between the United Kingdom and Australia, and her four masts were the tallest of any ship to pass under Sydney Harbour Bridge.

Details of her sinking are few, chiefly because only Eric Munday miraculously lived to tell the story of the horrors experienced by so many at that awful time. Although hit by about four or five torpedoes, Ceramic took an hour to die — alone and unescorted, west of the Azores in latitude 40.30 N, longitude 40.20 W. She was destroyed by the U.515, commanded by Kapitan-Leutnant Werner Henke, who was also credited with the sinking of seven other ships with a total tonnage of 45,255, off the West African coast on April 30/May 1 the following year . . . and many more.

Some idea of the weather conditions prevailing at that time can be gauged from other ships which were in that area. A former bosun of the Royal Mail Line freighter, Palma, Mr. Albert Murray told how his ship left Liverpool with a cargo of landmines, ammunition, tanks and aircraft for delivery to Russia, via the Cape and the Persian Gulf. And how, in the same stormy area as Ceramic, Palma's crew thought that they were being pursued by two U. boats.

"The Palma was a fast ship and we were not in convoy," he said. "That night, the chief engineer took the governors off the engines and let her go at full speed. The sea buried her. Raft frames and rafts disappeared over the side. Four fighter planes, in crates, ended up in shambles. But we got away from the submarines. It was then, during the worst and dirtiest night I ever remember at sea, that we picked up an S.O.S. from the Ceramic, saying that she had been torpedoed."

Palma turned back and for several hours fought the gale and huge seas in a fruitless search for the liner and her survivors. There was little doubt that she had sunk with all hands, and Palma finally received a radio message that she was to resume her passage. The Palma herself became a war victim on her very next voyage, when she was sunk in the Indian Ocean with the loss of many of her crew.

Ceramic's sinking was announced by Germany in the same month, but because of the uncertainty over survivors, it was not until ten months later that Britain confirmed this.

I am informed that two other ships with Merseyside connections were also sunk in the same area as Ceramic on the same night. These were the cargo vessel Peter Maersk (5,476 tons), of Elder Dempster Line, Liverpool, and the 5,026-ton Henry Stanley, a war transport and former Danish ship, managed by Moss Hutchinson Line, of Liverpool. The former's 56 crew and 11 passengers all perished, and only the master survived from the latter, being taken a prisoner on board the U. boat. The remainder of his ship's 52 crew and 12 passengers died.

There must have been many seamen in the last war who lived to "thank their lucky stars" because, for one reason or another, they were unable to join ships which were destined to die. And Ceramic's story would not be complete without one or two of these "near

Ceramic shares a quiet interlude with a sister of her line. (Furness Withy)

misses". Former able seamen Joseph B. Harthen, of Fazakerley, Liverpool, told me how he had been working by Ceramic for six weeks. But the night before he was due to sail in her from Liverpool on her last voyage, he "had a few" and, consequently, awoke too late next day to join her.

"I hurried down to the ship, only to see her sailing out of the lock," he said. "All my clothes were on board and I was left on the quay with a fireman, whose name, I think, was Frank Berry."

Joe got another ship, the grand liner Andes, and it was not until he returned to Liverpool from New York, with another small army of American troops, that he heard Ceramic had been sunk with the loss of many of his old shipmates. "I know that there were a lot of women on board Ceramic on that last trip," said Joe who, although in ships torpedoed before and after he signed on for the Ceramic, reckons that missing the latter ship "was the luckiest escape of my life."

Just as the Titanic had its witnesses to premonitions which stopped them from sailing with her on her ill-fated maiden voyage, Ceramic had at least one. Retired able seaman Dan Conroy, of Liverpool, who spent 45 years at sea, told me of that which he believed to be a supernatural occurence during the last war.

He had arranged to sign on for service with the Ceramic one Thursday, two voyages in advance of her final one, and was having breakfast when his landlady asked him what was the matter.

"I must have been feeling a bit fidgety for some reason I couldn't explain," said Dan, who told his landlady that he was going out that morning to sign on for duty with the Ceramic. She wished me luck and I went out of the back-kitchen into the yard with the intention of leaving by the back-entry door. This door was unlocked and only on the latch, but I could not budge it. I tried with all my might, but it seemed as if a strong power was barring my exit and I instinctively knew that it was preventing me from leaving for some good reason."

Dan, who experienced all the hell at sea during the Battle of the Atlantic, accepted this as a positive sign that he should not present himself at the ship. "I simply went back into the house and did not sign on for the Ceramic," he said. "And I was more than ever convinced of that strange warning when I learned that she had been sunk two voyages afterwards."

Mr. Cecil D'Aguiar, of Southampton, who might well have been on board Ceramic when she was sunk, told me that he owes his life to a simple incident. For almost a year he had been a catering steward in the liner and then left her because of his annoyance over a leave-draw.

The draw, for crew leave, was held in two parts. "My name," he explained, "was drawn with the first lot. But, when the lists were posted, my name was among those on the second list. This was done, I was told, because local men were to go on leave first. I thought, 'I'm not having this,' and left the ship, which was sunk two voyages later."

As one of the numerous Merseyside families bereaved when Ceramic sank, Mr. Peter Leacy, of Bootle, told me that because the liner employed so many local people, she was also known as a 'family boat'. "We all acknowledged that there were other, greater disasters in terms of life-loss," he said, "but in the context of the time in which Ceramic was destroyed, this was probably the biggest single, rivetting incident to reverberate for a long time afterwards in that mile-wide belt between the river and Everton Road . . . ."

* * *

What really did happen to Ceramic? Only Eric Munday returned to tell the tale. And, in the quietude of a sunlit Croydon park one summer day, 1,200 miles and 39 years away from the Ceramic's cold grave, he told me about his amazing escape . . . . in the killer submarine!

Sapper Eric Alfred Munday (2148743), aged 20, was stationed at Penarth, South Wales, with the Royal Engineers in 1942, when he and his friend, Jock Hayes, volunteered to join the 14th Army in Burma. They moved into a transit "camp" at the Great Central Hotel, Marylebone, London, as the only two R.E.'s among a group of about 100 other uniformed personnel, including the Royal Marines, Royal Corps of Signals, REME's, and about 80 members of the Queen Alexandra's Royal Army Nursing Corps. Eventually, they all travelled by train to Liverpool and boarded the S.S. Ceramic in dock. She was a splendid vessel, coping with passengers and cargo and not converted for trooping. She sailed on November 23.

Eric Munday – sole survivor.

For one and a half days before she sailed, the smokers on board played havoc because they could not obtain cigarettes, and their protests finally succeeded in having the bonded store opened for tobacco — and booze!

"Although we were service personnel, we were treated as civilian passengers, like the hundreds of whom were on board, including families travelling to Australia," said Eric. "At the start, the sea was smooth and the weather good. So was everything else for that matter. In fact, my friends and I were having the time of our lives — plenty of beer, whisky, cigarettes, women, entertainments and, above all, really good food. It was like returning to pre-war Britain! Everyone on board was in high spirits, especially the few military personnel. Jock and I were in a draft of 14 engineers, bound for somewhere in South or West Africa — the scheduled port of disembarkation I never knew."

Unlike most of the troops in those days, packed below decks in cramped quarters, with lash-up bunks and only small blue lamps for lighting, the servicemen were given their own cabins — and sumptuous food.

When the voyage began, the main saloon was given over to officers only and put out of bounds to other ranks. Another bar was opened for the latter — down below. "But we got our own back," Eric said. "A dance was organised, with all the nurses invited, but the officers excluded. Our retaliation worked, for the very next day the whole ship was thrown open to us!

"Our convoy sailed from Liverpool, round Northern Ireland, and on into the North Atlantic to Newfoundland. But we did not land there. Instead, Ceramic, being a fast ship, left the convoy and headed south to the Azores — alone. It was fairly hairy after leaving Liverpool and we started submarine and aircraft watch, doing shifts on the Oerliken guns. This, at least, gave us something to do and helped to relieve the boredom. The weather worsened and many on board were very seasick. On one occasion, my pal and I found that we were the only two at breakfast! The small escort vessels were being tossed about like corks. We were just getting our sea-legs, had made many friends among the passengers, and were looking forward to the warmer weather, when it all happened.

"On the night of December 6, I came off watch at 7.30, washed and changed and went up to the smoke-room to have a drink and to play cards. About 8 p.m., local time, I was playing solo with my friends.

Then, 15 minutes later, the first torpedo hit us. This was followed by two more at about five or ten-minute intervals. They were all on the starboard side of the ship — the first one forward and the other two, as far as I know, amidships. I learned later that two more were fired after an interval of about three hours.

"Emergency Stations" was sounded, followed almost immediately by "Boat Stations". Ceramic developed a heavy list to port. "It was quite dark outside and the sea was rough. It was also cold. The port-side boat stations' lights were lit, which made things a little easier, and the boats were starting to be lowered about half an hour after the first explosion. Fortunately, our lifeboat was on this side.

"I saw several boatloads of women get away. Most of the relatively little panic and confusion arose from the concern of parents to rescue their children, most of whom, because of the time, were in their cabins below.

"The boat that I eventually got into was in the water, so I had to drop down a rope, cutting my hands pretty badly in doing so. But the pain was quickly forgotten in the general excitement which, I thought afterwards, was quite accounted for. There were about 45 to 50 people in my boat. Two of them were women and the rest chiefly servicemen, because we had been assigned to that lifeboat during the routine drills. It is almost impossible to imagine that a ship of Ceramic's size, with women and children on board, could be abandoned with the ease of guardsmen drilling on a barracks square. But that was how it was."

In his diary (which he started writing on December 10, while in the U. boat) Eric recalls that they had difficulty in getting away from the side of the liner as the lifeboat falls caught on an obstruction.

The following hours of darkness were dreadful. "The sea, by 12 o'clock (midnight) was very heavy, with frequent downpours of rain," he wrote. "It was all we could do to keep her (the lifeboat) head on into the wind and bale the water out. Owing to a number of the lads being ill, I had to row right through the night," he said.

This made him very tired and his hands, already cut by the falls, were now blistered and skinned. But, at least, rowing kept him reasonably warm "and prevented me from lying down and thinking about what lay ahead." His diary continues . . . .

"7 December: The night seemed endless, but when at last the daylight came we saw quite a few rafts around us and we were able to exchange a few words with one another. About 8 a.m., the wind got up and the storm started. It was impossible to keep our boat head on into the wind, so we just let it drift and concentrated on the baling . . ."

Eric said that other seamen, who had been in the vicinity at the time, had said later that this storm was one of the worst they had experienced.

"It was too much to expect help that day, but I did not wish another night in this weather, as the rain chilled me to the bone, but on the whole, I felt cheerful and confident that we could hold out — that is, if things did not get worse."

Eric wrote that it was impossible to describe his thoughts at this time. But having been a regular churchgoer and former boy chorister, he certainly knew how to pray. He told how he asked "that Mum and Dad would not worry about me," and that he thanked them all for what they had done for him . . . . also, that Norman (his younger brother) would be spared the war, and that his other brothers, Ron, in the Royal Engineers, and Doug, in the Tank Regiment, would soon be back home.

Then came the final disaster . . . . "I was sitting forward on the starboard side when the boat capsized and I was first into the water. The others, coming out on top of me, prevented me from reaching the surface. I really did feel scared, but at last there was a gap and I came up. The lads were clambering over the upturned boat but there were too many on one side and over it went again. I did not attempt to get on because I thought it would never again be seaworthy. I began searching for a raft, but all I could find were a few pieces of wood, which were very helpful.

"I saw quite a number of people drown and there were a lot of bodies in the water, supported by their life-jackets," Eric told me during our interview.

"I was now all on my own and the storm seemed worse. I could see the lifeboat some way off and made my way towards it. Jock and Ramsbottom were two whom I recognised, so I hung on. The next thing I saw was a big shape in the water about 100 yards away. The waves were so big though that we only saw it for a few seconds. I immediately swam in that direction, and after a couple of minutes I saw it again. This time I could see it was a submarine.

"I felt very happy and wanted to shout and laugh, but my hardest job was getting alongside. One time, I was so near I could see the faces of the men in the conning tower. The next minute, I was swept right away and I thought that the submarine had submerged. But after another few minutes I saw it again and made one last effort to reach it. I got alongside and two sailors each threw a rope to me. I missed them both. They threw again and this time I managed to hold one. One of them caught hold of my hand and then I was on the boat — a German U. boat . . . .

"They gave me some food and dry clothing and then fixed me up with a hammock. I was feeling quite well but very tired. Our time, 1200 hours."

Ceramic, sailing in smooth, peacetime waters.

Eric was picked up by the U. 515, which sank the Ceramic.

Kapitan Henke said in an interview long afterwards how he brought the U. boat to the surface at 11 a.m. on December 7 in rain and hail. He had orders from his h.q. to find out where the Ceramic had been bound and returned to the site of the sinking to try and find her captain. The U. boat was still searching at 1.30 p.m. when he had lunch, and by the time he had returned to the bridge, the wind had increased to Force 10 and the sea was almost swamping the conning tower.

The lookout on the submarine saw a body, then empty life-jackets and a broken mast. Then they saw a lifeboat with some occupants who waved to them. They had reached the area of the sinking.

Henke said that he was very upset at the sights, but steeled himself by thinking about one of his former crew. This man had been killed whilst manning the deck gun in a previous engagement and Henke had had to crash dive suddenly, leaving the sailor's body lashed in a net on deck. At the subsequent burial, Henke was seen to cry and said aloud "Bloody war!".

A rubber dinghy floated near U. 515. Among its mostly male occupants was a woman holding a young child in her arms. Her hair was dishevelled and hanging over her eyes. Henke was disturbed by the scene and his hands shook.

"We'll take the first one to come nearest to us," he shouted to his crew and, for a moment, thought how crazy it was that he should be playing God by choosing one to survive among so many.

When the two oilskin-clad sailors on the U. boat's deck — held by ropes from the bridge — saw a uniformed man swimming towards them, they threw ropes to him and one bent down to the water's edge and grabbed him . . . . Private Eric Munday was hauled on board.

As Eric lay like a wet sack on tne heaving iron deck, the Germans at first thought he had died. His neck was bright red from the long chafing of uniform and salt water. His hands were swollen and bloodied from rowing and immersion. But the young, strong Englishman still clung to life. He was half carried into the conning tower and taken below.

At 5.35 p.m., U. 515 submerged into the silent world below the waves, leaving behind the nightmare scenes above.

Eric was given medical attention by one of the crew who had taken a first-aid course. He was questioned by those who spoke a little English but could not tell them for where Ceramic had been bound because he didn't know himself. His army paybook told the Germans that he belonged to the Royal Engineers and he said that his unit had consisted of only 50 men. The Germans could not understand why troops, woman and children were in the same ship.

Eric continues with his diary . . . .

* * *

"*8 December:* I awoke feeling very sore and aching so much that I could hardly move. In a day or so though it wore off. Everything was very strange and besides feeling none too good, I felt very depressed. In the evening, the Commandant and presumably the First Officer, questioned me as to movements of the Ceramic."

He tells how he was given a toothbrush and a comb but could not use these for days because of his bandaged hands. He was allowed a cigarette only occasionally and permitted to go on deck for fresh air ("it was like a million dollars") only every few days.

On December 12, he spent his 21st birthday on U. 515 — "one vastly different to the one I had meant to have," he wrote . . . . "I was allowed some air and time to smoke two cigarettes." He also notes the irony of the Germans' frequently tuning in their radio to listen to British programmes including 'jazz and Bobby Howes'. "On one occasion," said Eric, "when the British National Anthem was being played, the set was switched off rather hurriedly!"

A piece of news he didn't pick up was that on December 20, when Henke was informed by radio that he had been awarded the Iron Cross for his actions at sea.

The young soldier spent Christmas and New Year on the submarine. The former was quite reasonable, considering the circumstances, he said, and the Germans made piles of cream from some of the 50 cases of New Zealand butter which they had recently found floating and had fished out of the sea.

Of Christmas Eve, he writes: "About six o'clock, all the lights were

112

turned off and they lit a small Christmas tree; it was very effective. Then they sang songs, equivalent, I believe, to our carols because one of them was to the tune of our carol, 'Silent Night'. We drank hot punch and ate chocolate and biscuits and also a piece of thickly-creamed sponge-cake. They gave me a present of some chocolate. No air or smoke."

For Christmas dinner next day, Eric had some tinned chicken, potatoes and four half-peaches from a can. "Smoked two cigarettes and have not seen daylight since the 17th," he wrote. "I smoke on a platform just before reaching the top."

U. 515 tied up at its pen in Lorient on January 6, 1943, and Eric was taken ashore to join five Englishmen brought in by other U. boats — but none was from the Ceramic. They were a ship's master, two majors, a captain and a flying officer. "Admiral Doenitz was also on the quayside to meet us," said Eric.

He recalls having been treated well while on board the U. 515 — particularly by the younger crewmen, who saw that he got adequate rations and who warned him to stay clear of one of the officers who, they said, was an S.S. man. "They also explained to me that they had tried to pick up another survivor — presumably hoping he would be the Ceramic's captain — and I think that had they managed to rescue an officer, I would have been thrown back!"

The U. boat's crew gave Eric some tins of butter to take with him, but these were confiscated when he went ashore. The prisoners were then taken on a 36-hour train journey to a barracks in Wilhelmshaven for interrogation, arriving there on January 8.

A month later, Eric was removed to a p.o.w. camp — Stalag VIII B, at Wallamsdorf, near Breslau, where his diary was stamped and returned to him. Later, he was removed to another camp in Sudetenland, were Red Cross parcels were delivered. His mother and father, Mr. and Mrs. Ernest Munday, had a telegram about three weeks after the Ceramic sank, to say that Eric was missing presumed drowned. They only learned that he had survived after someone had heard his broadcast via "Germany Calling" — transmitted from Calais on February 17, 1943, in a programme called "The Battle of the Seven Seas".

Survivors had been told that they would be allowed to give their names, ranks and numbers over the air and to say that they were safe and well. "I suspect this was done as an obvious method of getting us to virtually confirm that certain ships had been sunk by the Germans," said Eric.

In one of the first notes he wrote as a p.o.w., Eric said: "I consider myself to be one of the luckiest persons to be alive today. After being in the water two or three hours, I was picked up by the U. boat. This can only be described as an act of God and nothing else."

Sequel to this story is that as the end of the war in Europe neared, Sapper Munday was among other prisoners, being marched with a column of Germans, from their camp towards the western lines, in order to avoid the advancing Russian troops. With a small group of prisoners, he managed to escape into Czechoslovakia, and they were eventually told to make for a castle at Kysperk, where the aristocratic Schnehen family would give them sanctuary. They were duly accepted and received food and shelter from May 8 to May 29, 1945. One of the family, they were told — Count von Stubenberg — was a prisoner of war in England!

This postcard, showing the Ceramic, was dated April 15, 1937, and addressed to Mrs. Elford, Captain Elford's wife. It was sent by the company (Shaw, Savill and Albion) to confirm that the liner had arrived at Durban the day before.

When the Russians arrived in the town, they were told that the British soldiers had taken over the castle. "They left us alone," said Eric, "but when the Mayor told us it would be wise to move on, we caught one of the first trains to Prague. As we were late, the lines of communications were closed. So, some of the Aussies in our company pinched a lorry and we drove through to the American lines at Pilsen. The Americans then flew us to Paris and the R.A.F. returned us to England."

After a joyful but tearful reunion with his family, Eric had the tough task of visiting Captain Elford's widow in Finchley, London, and relating the grim story of the sinking all over again.

When the Ceramic's fate became known, Eric's mother, Mrs. Moyra Munday, started to receive letters from all over the world. There were some 800 of these, written by relatives and friends of those who had died in the tragedy. "Many more hundreds of letters were sent to me, too, in 1945," says Eric, who adds: "My mother struck up many friendships as a result of this correspondence, and she even received regular food parcels from a mother living in South Africa who had lost her son in the war."

Today, happily married, with his wife, Joan, three daughters and two sons, and a proud grandfather too, Eric still marvels at why he alone among some 656 souls was destined to live.

* * *

What Kapitan-Leutnant Werner Henke, Knight's Cross with Oak Leaves, had done must have haunted him for the rest of the relatively short life he had left. He had fired torpedoes into a ship with virtually no chance of retaliating, had surfaced and witnessed the most appalling scenes of drowning men, women and children, some of the latter still clutched by their mothers.

Henke didn't order an S.O.S., which might eventually have brought rescue ships and saved many of the victims. Seizing the fortunate Sapper Munday — a uniformed man, who might have had some useful information to impart — he closed the conning tower on the horrible scene and dived into the untroubled depths, with desperate drowning men still clinging to the ironwork in flurries of foam . . . .

Such was the picture the Allies painted of Henke. Certainly, the Americans were very incensed over the incident. They accused him of murder and called him a war criminal.

It was alleged that Sapper Munday was asked to broadcast to make out that the U. boat commander was really a compassionate man

Henke, however, always insisted that he had suffered a gross injustice for his conduct at sea and adamantly declared that he had constantly adhered strictly to the international codes of war conduct. He claimed that he sank the Ceramic because she was blacked out, operating in the war zone and was recognised as an armed merchantman.

U. 515 finally paid for all her "killings" by her own death, off Madeira, on April 9, 1944 , when attacked by aircraft from the U.S. escort carrier, Guadalcanal, and then by American destroyers. Henke and his crew of 43 were rescued and taken prisoner to the United States where, some months later, Henke was shot dead by security guards while attempting to escape.

The Germans naturally made some useful propaganda from this incident by declaring that Henke was murdered.

115

Circassia (II), Cilicia & Caledonia

A great favourite on the Liverpool-India run, Circassia (II) sailed in peace and war for nearly 30 years.   (Anchor Line)

The crew of a brand-new ship on her trials might well have construed as a bad omen a radio report that a sinking vessel lay on their course. For the 11,500-ton motorship Circassia (II), on passage from the Clyde to Liverpool before sailing on her maiden voyage to Bombay, received the message:

"Clan liner disabled and abandoned off Mersey Bar ...." and, shortly afterwards, sighted the stricken ship, the Clan Mackenzie, now settled, with only masts and funnel tops showing above the water.

But the young Circassia, whose illustrious Anchor Line fleet lineage went back to 1854, had long and fruitful years ahead of her. In fact, the chairman of Anchor Line, Mr. Philip Runciman, on board at that time, had a much more cheerful declaration to make. "This ship is our message to Liverpool. What finer message could we send to any port?" he said.

And so Circassia announced herself to Liverpool, her regular port for most of her life.

A splendid, black-hulled liner, with red boot-topping, tiers of white decks and a single black funnel, she was one of a trio with which the company hoped to establish a first-class, 20-day service from Liverpool to Bombay and Karachi. Built by Fairfield's, of Glasgow, Circassia was launched on June 8, 1937. Cilicia, her sister, was launched the next November and the trio would have been completed by the improved Britannia — then on the Liverpool-India service — but for the outbreak of war.

Anchor liner Circassia in Alexandra Dock, Liverpool, loading and embarking passengers prior to starting her maiden voyage on October 28, 1937.

Circassia's maiden voyage from Liverpool took place on October 28, 1937. Spectators, who had assembled at Prince's Landing Stage to see her depart, were disappointed. Late with loading, she sailed with her passengers straight from the Alexandra Dock, under the command of Captain William Gemmell.

During the war (when she carried 75,000 troops), Circassia flew the White Ensign as an armed merchant cruiser until March, 1942, when she was refitted as a troopship. She was engaged in the Sicilian landings in co-operation with American naval units and was commanded by Captain (later Sir) David Bone at the Salerno invasion and also took part in the south of France landings in 1944. Following in the wake of Cilicia, which did a similar wartime job, she returned to "Civvy Street" in May, 1947.

While anchored in the Mersey on the 12th of that month, her crew saved the lives of six Sea Cadets and their three officers when their cutter fouled the side of the liner and threw them all into the river.

At Birkenhead in August, 1948, she was reconverted to a passenger liner. She and her new sister, the 11,315-ton Caledonia (V), which made her maiden voyage in April that year, joined with Cilicia to maintain a regular service from the Mersey to India.

Caledonia (V), which made regular sailings from Liverpool to the Far East, ended up as a hostel for Amsterdam University. (Anchor Line)

Among Circassia's 298 first class passengers, who sailed from Liverpool to India in September, 1948, were the 60 members of the Indian Olympic team; H.H. the Maharini of Nawanager and family, and Sir Ness Wadia, a wealthy 75-years-old Bombay millowner, on his 99th trip between India and Britain.

Ten years on, in March, 1958, the liner arrived at Liverpool flying the Yellow Jack, the quarantine flag. Professor Andrew B. Semple, then Liverpool's Medical Officer of Health, went on board and confirmed smallpox in a Lascar seaman. A team of doctors vaccinated some 300 of the liner's passengers and crew of 145.

And seven years later, Anchor Line announced the withdrawal and disposal of the three sister-ships. This was a dramatic statement because it heralded the end of the Company's regular passenger service to India, which had lasted 110 years.

Anchor Line was a prominent and vital link between Britain and India at the time when the latter represented such an important part of the British Empire. Their ships carried eight Indian princes, who were guests at the coronation of King George V1. And, many years earlier, at the time of the Indian Mutiny, they had carried British troops. In 1869, the Anchor liner, Dido, was the first British merchant ship to sail through the Suez Canal.

Among Circassia's passengers on her last 13,000-mile voyage from Birkenhead to India, under Captain Angus Colquhoun, was the company's retiring passenger traffic manager, Mr. Menzies Paterson, who had sailed with her on her maiden voyage in 1937.

Circassia, pictured at Birkenhead on January 13, 1966, a few hours before she sailed on her last round voyage to Bombay, early the following day.

How ships can cast a spell on some of their passengers is instanced by the reaction of one, Mr. Tommy Marsden. Until 1962, a director of two textile mills in India, Tom, of Brookhouse, near Lancaster, said on the occasion of this nostalgic departure that a member of his family had sailed in one or another of the Anchor Line ships every year since 1910. "When I heard of this last voyage, I decided that I must be on board to maintain the family tradition," he said.

Hundreds of dockers, seamen and other spectators bid Circassia goodbye as she left Ballard Pier, Bombay, for her last run home, flying a long, white pennant — traditional on farewell voyages. A police band played her out, but this was nothing to the send-off she received from Merseyside after she docked at Birkenhead to disembark passengers and discharge her cargo. British Rail, which had run special trains for Anchor liners' passengers for the past 16 years, arranged a full-scale Scottish farewell for the ship.

Circassia's 300 passengers and 187 crew, who came ashore on March 15, 1966, were greeted at the quayside by 60-years-old Wallasey Piper, David Renton, of the Liverpool Clan McLeod Pipe Band, who played the traditional "Will Ye No Come Back Again?" But Circassia was not to see the Mersey again.

One of the last passengers to leave her was Lord Sinha, of Raipur, who made the same trip for the previous 20 years to take his seat in the House of Lords.

Mr. P.V.K. Christie, the Indian Consul in Liverpool, said that Anchor Line had always had the utmost consideration and regard for their Indian crews, who had formed the majority of the catering staff on board their vessels.

Tribute also came from Liverpool's Lord Mayor. Alderman David Cowley had a special reason for regretting the ending of Anchor Line's passenger service, and he said: ".... it was in Anchor Line's

And here she is at the end of that voyage, on March 15, 1966, at Prince's Landing Stage, Liverpool, where Scottish piper, Dave Renton, of Wallasey, played the lament, "Will ye no come back again?"

120

Britannia that I came home after being torpedoed during the war. They treated me with the greatest kindness imaginable, and I shall always be grateful to them."

That afternoon, Captain Colquhoun ("This is one of the saddest days of my life"), who had served the company for 30 years, stood in with the driver of the boat-train, which took some 120 passengers on to London. The train was waved away with an Anchor Line flag instead of the usual guard's green flag!

Again, we heard how economics had forced the company to end the service. It would have cost Anchor Line £5 million to replace Circassia and the passenger potential was no longer there to justify the outlay.

Circassia left Birkenhead for Glasgow on March 25. She had a last little fling with a cruise in Scottish waters, carrying present and past directors of the company, and then she sailed to the breaker's yard at Alicante, and into oblivion.

Captain Angus Colquhoun (centre) is pictured at Liverpool with, left to right, Mr. C.A. Dove, director general of the Mersey Docks and Harbour Board; Mr. P.V.K. Christie, Indian Consul in Liverpool; the Lord Mayor of Liverpool, Alderman David Cowley, and Lord Sinha, of Raipur, one of the passengers on Circassia's last voyage from Bombay, who had made regular trips from India to Britain for 20 years to sit in the House of Lords.

* * *

Cilicia, launched at Glasgow on November 21, 1937, was virtually pitched into the war before she had time to make any pre-war passenger-service history. She made her maiden voyage to Bombay in June, 1938. On August 3, 1939, she was taken over by the Admiralty and served as an armed merchant cruiser for four and a half years.

But she and Caledonia (V), which replaced Britannia in the India-run trio ten years later (making her maiden voyage from Liverpool to Bombay in April, 1948), soon made up that leeway in their post-war voyages. They carried hundreds of colourful personalities among the thousands of passengers moving to and from the Far East.

Only two months after Caledonia's maiden voyage, Cilicia helped Liverpool to clock up another of the "firsts", of which it boasts so many. Nothing for the Guinness Book of Records, perhaps, but still she became the first ship on which a waste-paper baling-machine was fitted — by the Lord Mayor of Liverpool, on June 23, 1948! Another claim to fame was that, in 1965, Tristan Da Cunha's 6d stamp bore her picture, showing her in her wartime role of H.M.S. Cilicia, the armed merchant cruiser. Up to that period, anyway, this was the only stamp ever issued showing a merchant ship in this capacity.

The story behind this honour was that the liner had played an important part in the installation of a meteorological station on Tristan — an operation known as "Job 9". Naval personnel selected to man the station were permitted by the Amiralty to take their wives and families with them to this lovely island, eventually to be nicknamed "HMS Atlantic Isle". It presented a big headache for the planners, who had to consign a veritable township, from dwellings to babies' nappies, to this outpost! Cilicia carried most of this mixed cargo in her capacious holds and, although she was at the island from May 9 to June 9, 1942, only seven days were favourable for landing.

In May, 1947, she was completely overhauled and refitted and returned to the Liverpool-Bombay run, joining Castalia II and Tarantia III.

Cilicia's and Caledonia's Far Eastern service, like that of Circassia, ended in 1965, when they, too, were put up for sale. Caledonia went to Amsterdam that December and was used by the city's university as a hostel. She was finally removed to Hamburg in 1971 and broken up. Cilicia, renamed Jan Backx, went to Rotterdam and became a school for stevedores and engineering apprentices, until August, 1980, when she was towed out of Rotterdam on her way to Bilbao to be broken up.

Britannia (III) . . . lost her master, 14 officers, 89 Indian ratings and 12 European passengers, when fired at and sunk by an armed raider in March, 1941. (Anchor Line)

An interesting war story concerns Cilicia and Britannia (III) .... Britannia had left Liverpool on March 12, 1941, sailing alone, and when some 720 miles west of Freetown, at 7.45 a.m. on the 25th, she sighted another vessel. Playing safe, she altered course. The unidentified, faster vessel, chased her and opened fire on her. Britannia dropped smoke-flares, increased speed and also returned the raider's fire.

The liner's gunners managed to loose off a dozen rounds before an enemy shell killed or disabled them and put their gun out of action. Britannia was then hit again. Her boat-deck aft was on fire and the first-class smoking-room in flames. Most of her lifeboats were damaged by splinters.

Although Britannia's master signalled that he was abandoning ship, the raider fired another five rounds at the liner — two of the shells finding their mark. After she was abandoned, the raider sank her and then cleared off at high speed, making no attempt to pick up any survivors.

Britannia lost her master, 14 officers, 89 Indian ratings and 12 European passengers.

Dr. A. Nancy Miller was on board Britannia for that grim voyage, making her first trip to sea as surgeon. Her father, Dr. Thomas Miller, was surgeon in the Cilicia. So, when the latter heard about Britannia's· sinking, he spent three nightmarish days wondering about his daughter's fate.

Nancy was in a lifeboat with 63 other survivors. She was the last to climb in. Eventually, they were all picked up by the Spanish steamer, Bachi.

At 6.25 a.m. on the 28th, Cilicia sighted a small steamer and sent a boarding party to investigate her. She was the Bachi. By 9.30 a.m., the survivors from Britannia were alongside Cilicia .... and first on deck (this time) was Nancy, who was hugged by her overjoyed father. The survivors were landed at Freetown a couple of days later.

According to the citation in the London Gazette of February 17, 1942, Dr. Nancy Miller, "with perfect calm, attended to the wounded and dying. She continued her good work after the ship's company had taken to the boats and by her efforts saved many lives."

Built in 1925, the 17,000-ton M.V. Caledonia (IV), made her maiden voyage from Glasgow to New York on October 3 that year. She became an armed merchant cruiser from the outbreak of the last world war, was renamed Scotstoun and was torpedoed by a U.boat on June 13, 1940.

(Hutchinson, Liverpool)

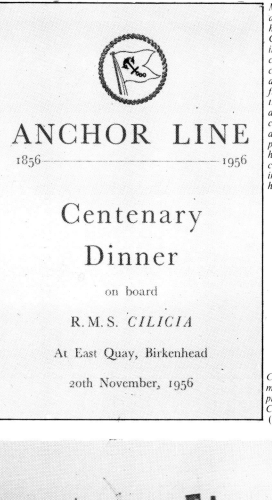

ANCHOR LINE

1856 ———————————— 1956

Centenary
Dinner

on board

R.M.S. *CILICIA*

At East Quay, Birkenhead

20th November, 1956

Menu cover for the dinner (haggis and all!) held on board the Cilicia at Birkenhead in November, 1956, to celebrate Anchor Line's centenary. Representatives of Merseyside firms connected with the company since the arrival of its first clipper from Bombay, at the end of 1855, were present. Cilicia also hosted a similar centenary celebration in Glasgow, the line's headquarters.

Cilicia, as an armed merchant cruiser, pictured off Tristan da Cunha, in June, 1942. (Merseyside Maritime Museum)

The former Cilicia, renamed Jan Backx, photographed at Rotterdam, where she served as a dockers' training ship. Behind her is the vessel, "Seven Seas".
(Merseyside Maritime Museum)

Calm waters for Cilicia in her peacetime role.
(Merseyside Maritime Museum)

Seacats

Ever since Britannia ruled the waves, to the present (when she still helps out!) cats have been associated with ships.

They were also considered to be lucky mascots and not a vessel could safely put to sea without one. And, said the old-time sailors, killing a cat would surely lead to disaster.

Some sailors swore that these intelligent creatures made excellent barometers. They believed that when a cat clawed its way up the weatherside of the forerigging that a gale was on its way. And that a cat licking its fur the wrong way meant adverse winds.

* * *

Captain Sir Arthur Rostron loved cats. For many years, his pet, Abdul, a long-haired, pure white (and deaf) persian, travelled the oceans with him. At New Year, 1929, the dockside fraternity all along the shores of the Hudson River were wondering if they would see Abdul taking his customary stroll ashore on the end of his lead, when his ship, the Mauretania, arrived from England. The feeling was that, if the old cat was still listed among Maurie's complement, then he would be unable to disembark without submitting to the indignity of six months' quarantine under the new regulations of the British Board of Agriculture, which came into effect that New Year's Day ...

* * *

Two small brass plates — fixed on each side of a white star, on a dainty red collar, with enamel badges bearing the ship's name at either end — tell another tale of a ship's pet. . . . .

"I am Doodles," reads the inscription. "I was born in 1927 on the White Star Liner Cedric, in which I travelled over 360,000 miles."

The souvenir collar was presented by the White Star Line to Mr. H. Hutton, of the Marquis of Granby Hotel, Bamford, Derbyshire, where Doodles was taken to live in forced retirement. Doodles had refused to leave the Cedric when she left Liverpool for the last time and sucessfully evaded capture until the ship arrived at Inverkeithing to be broken up. After leading a very miserable life there for some time, following workmen about and meowing piteously, someone took good care of her and gave her a new home at the hotel.

* * *

And how's this for yet another matelot-moggie memory — a story told in November, 1945, when the Empress of Scotland arrived at Liverpool from Bombay with serviceman returning from India.

Smoky, the ship's cat, went ashore in Liverpool when the liner was in that port three months earlier and just on the point of leaving for India. Presumably, the call of the city's warehouses and alley cats must have been strong, for Smoky failed to report for duty at sailing time and was posted as missing, presumed lost. But, six weeks later, as the Empress was preparing to depart from Bombay, to the astonishment of the crew, who should come nonchalantly sauntering along the quay, up the gangway and into the ship, but Smoky!

* * *

One of the strangest sea-cat yarns concerns the puss which once belonged to the ill-fated Empress of Ireland.

Some minutes before the liner sailed from Liverpool for what was to be the last time, the ship's cat, which had lived on board for two years, ran down the gangway. A sailor recovered her, but she escaped again and ran back to the quayside and disappeared into a shed. As the liner was departing, the cat reappeared among the crowd of people on shore who were waving farewell. . . . .